Groan in the Throat Vol. 1

Groan in the Throat Vol. 1

"White Supremacy Is a Religion" and Other Essays on Being Black, Keeping the Faith, and Surviving America

TONY BAUGH

Foreword by James Henry Harris

WIPF & STOCK · Eugene, Oregon

GROAN IN THE THROAT VOL. 1
"White Supremacy Is a Religion" and Other Essays on Being Black, Keeping the Faith, and Surviving America

Copyright © 2021 Tony Baugh. All rights reserved. Except for brief quotations in critical publications or reviews, no part of this book may be reproduced in any manner without prior written permission from the publisher. Write: Permissions, Wipf and Stock Publishers, 199 W. 8th Ave., Suite 3, Eugene, OR 97401.

Wipf & Stock
An Imprint of Wipf and Stock Publishers
199 W. 8th Ave., Suite 3
Eugene, OR 97401

www.wipfandstock.com

PAPERBACK ISBN: 978-1-7252-9906-1
HARDCOVER ISBN: 978-1-7252-9907-8
EBOOK ISBN: 978-1-7252-9908-5

07/28/21

I dedicate this work to all my students at Nansemond River High School (2015–2018) in Suffolk, Virginia, and Woodrow Wilson High School (2019–2020) in Portsmouth, Virginia, for their spirit, their optimism, and their belief in me. You propped me up.

This is for all of us—for all the Black bodies still oppressed, deadened, and triumphant in a nameless system, and those who would ally themselves to our cause.

Contents

Foreword by James Henry Harris	ix
Acknowledgments	xiii
1. Introduction	3
2. On a Summer Being Stolen	12
3. Preaching and Justice	15
4. Slavoj Žižek and Being Racially Profiled	44
Interlude	49
5. White Supremacy Is a Religion	51
Addendum (January 6, 2021)	79
6. To My Sweet Boy	82
7. A Theology of Rejoicing	87
Coda	108
Glossary	111
Bibliography	113

Foreword

I am elated that Tony Baugh's thoughts are now in print for all who value reading and thinking to avail themselves of the opportunity to explore these powerful and insightful pages. Tony grew up in the pastor's house and in the fervent incubation of the Black church. They both provide a unique understanding and appreciation of Black life. In addition to that, he was able to negotiate the mean streets of Portsmouth, Virginia, and survive the racist taunts and the deliberate and demeaning acts of evil perpetrated against him and countless other Black males and females by the white police brigades in Tidewater, Virginia—a sample of Black life all over the United States. The miracle is that he has survived to write about it, while so many other Black men have not. This book is a mixtape, a new type of blending of concepts, an amalgamation of the literary and the philosophical, the theoretical and the practical. It reminds me, in a sense, of my own works *Black Suffering* and *No Longer Bound*. In that sense, the author is seeking to advance and expand knowledge and understanding beyond the strictures and structures of existing categories and classifications. You must read this work with an eye toward wonder and an open mind while sipping on a smooth glass of quality wine. A hot cup of coffee or tea will have the same affect for appreciating its depth and complexity. Tony writes with the ease and eye of an artist such as a Black conscious rapper like 2Pac, Mos Def, Erykah Badu, Talib Kweli, or a Black painter like Norman Lewis, Elizabeth Catlett, Thornton Dial, and Alma Thomas. These are the amalgam, the aesthetics, and the metaxological elements of style and creative art that this book embodies.

    The book is exemplary of memoir, as seen in the opening short story "On a Summer Being Stolen." The story itself is riveting yet ordinary, by which I mean normative, which makes it profound in the book's context. The author expresses some of the everyday fears and frustrations of being Black in America. Indeed, a nightmare. It's a struggle for survival because any white police officer or white citizen, for that matter, is too often looking to taunt, terrorize, traumatize, harass, mistreat, dehumanize, and/or murder a Black man or woman on any given day for any reason—which amounts to no reason at all. This is the tragedy and the fear that engulf the Black community in 2021, 402 years after 1619. Clearly, this white supremacy is America's religion, which is the central thesis of the book. I think that the U. S. Constitution is white America's God. Racism is her religion. This book explains so eloquently and systematically that major argument.

The element of letter writing, a type of focused, succinct memoir, is sad and somber, as evidenced by "To My Sweet Boy." It's a call to consciousness. When I read it, I can only compare it to James Baldwin's letter to his nephew in *The Fire Next Time*, which is a mapping of racism and oppression to a young Black child and to his brother (a grown man), as well as to himself. Tony Baugh expresses the same spirit to his high school student(s), who are clobbered every day by the public education system of injustice and hatred of the Black mind and body. Tony writes with the same passion and eloquence as Baldwin. Moreover, the letter is also akin to Ta-Nehisi Coates's *Between the World and Me* in both form and substance. This short letter in this short collection of essays and stories speaks volumes and creates a wellspring of emotion and empathy in my heart and soul. Whenever I read, reread, and unread it, I come away with tears in my eyes, burdened by deep sorrow and aghast at my own reflexive reaction. That's the power of his written words. Tony writes, "As you know, I am very fond of words—their . . . significations are my morning's salutation and my evening's rest. Yet . . . I cannot . . . put to paper all that this, my departing, has evoked. . . . gratitude . . . thankfulness." Wow. This is poetics and *poiesis* all wrapped into a univocal idea. To me, this is Black love, an almost wordless love by one who is a master linguist, a wordsmith as adept as J. L. Austin or Martin Luther King, Jr., or Maya Angelou or Sonia Sanchez.

This means that I read the words of Tony's letter with a gripping sadness that emanates from or is grounded in love—the love of Blackness. The entire book is a love letter. The letter is beyond Plato's *Symposium*. Unlike Plato's piece, this is not a contest of speeches by the likes of Socrates, Alcibiades, and Aristophanes. It is not sexual or erotic in any way like the Greek characters in the *Symposium*, but it is philosophical and cultural, which is why I prefer comparing it to Paul's discourse on love in 1 Corinthians 13. How else can I interpret this language, "Your dreams (this is my final lesson for you), your dreams—never let them die." This single line alone is the embodiment of the faith, hope, and love, which Tony Baugh, the consummate Socratic and Du Boisian teacher of youth, demonstrates throughout this book.

Paul of Tarsus writes a symposium-like letter to the Corinthians, which sums up his teaching as vicar of Christ: "And now faith, hope, and love abide, these three, and the greatest of these is love." These three ethical, philosophical, and practical actions are tied together in a way that means they cannot be disentangled or disengaged. Faith, hope, and love are inextricably and eternally linked and bonded together like the birds and the bees; like three peas in a pod; like the three stooges—Larry, Curly, and Moe; like the numbers one, two, and three—uno, dos, tres; faith, hope, and love. And, yet as I read Tony Baugh's book and watch the news, I see what can only be described as a hopeless tribe of individuals who seem to have given themselves over to the wiles of the devil—racism and white supremacy as religion, abuse, egoism, greed, and the destruction of the Black body, while exalting and glorying white supremacy, white evangelicalism—isn't this the godless religion that Tony Baugh reflects on? Every time I hear of a crime committed against another Black person, a police shooting of another person of my same Black complexion, the same slave heritage whose ancestors were Harriet Tubman and Sojourner Truth, I become nauseated. Every time I see a Black man or woman murdered by police, a person whose great-great-grandfathers and mothers were freedom fighters, educators, and preachers—folks like W. E. B. Du Bois, Booker T. Washington, Mary McLeod Bethune, and Fannie Lou Hamer—folk who worked from sunup to sundown—those who labored long and hard under physical and emotional duress and distress, under the searing heat of the sun and the scorching sizzle of summer's long and endless days, I cry all over again. In my imaginative anamnestic self, I can hear the ancestors in their southern dialects saying, "We done done all that us can do, now we must put our fate in the hands of God"—that's faith. That's hope. That's love. And, this is very much the spirit of what Tony Baugh's book is about. Everything in the book redounds toward a deep and abiding love for Black people, a written testimony in multiple linguistic forms.

Like the Corinthians, there are those who feel that knowledge is a sign of superiority—but knowledge of science and of art is still not enough to make white religion anything more than a racist construct and practice—a tribute to white supremacy. Martin Luther King, Jr., implied the same thing in his "Letter from Birmingham Jail" when he wrote, "I have looked at the South's beautiful churches with their lofty spires pointing heavenward.... 'Who is their God?'"

There is a nexus—a necessary relationship between faith, hope, and love. There is a powerful permanence to these three ethical, spiritual, and practical virtues. A permanence not seen in white evangelical religion. Tony Baugh makes it clear that the only visible permanence in white religion is racism—white supremacy. It seems to me that faith and hope need love in order to be transformative, and there's no evidence of agapeic love in the evil and hatred displayed toward Black people in the culture and religion of the white church from 1619 to 2021. Faith, hope, and love are the stalwarts of New Testament theology, yet visibly and intentionally absent in the white church and its state-sponsored religion. These three are what will turn the tide of violence and hatred in our communities and transform us from a battlefield of destruction and despair to an oasis of brotherhood. Love is tied to faith and hope, but love has no equal, as evidenced throughout this book. It exceeds faith, and it surpasses hope.

Let's be clear here. While Tony's book is all about love, white religion and American democracy are not. The ethical tenets of faith, hope, and love are anathema to the lived religion of whites. How else could the white church in America own and trade Blacks as slaves unless white supremacy obviated faith, hope, and love *vis-à-vis* justice and righteousness. The slavocracy, the murders of Blacks for 400 years, and American exceptionalism are the racist rituals that characterize white supremacy as a religion. Tony lays out how these ritualistic acts of hatred by white folk constitute their religion. He states, "This religion of white supremacy was established with its own liturgics long ago: slavery was really a kind of invocation, an opening prayer or hymn." The book lays out the reasoning and rationale for this groundbreaking thesis and explains how it continues today in the ritualistic murders of folk like Michael Brown, George Floyd, and Breonna Taylor. These systemic practices of evil toward Blacks constitute white folks' religion as a disembodied faith, and the white church, the White House, the constitution, the government, the university, the white family are all participants in this ritual of white supremacy as America's religion. As you read the book, your eyes will begin to open with renewed vision, and you too will see that this book is Tony's contribution to Black love, Black life.

JAMES HENRY HARRIS
Richmond, Virginia

Acknowledgments

I thank my God for giving me a voice and allowing that this, my first collection of essays, should be published.

I want to extend great gratitude to the good people at Wipf & Stock for believing in this project, particularly my editor Matthew Wimer and copyeditor Rebecca Abbott for their tireless efforts in helping me realize this publication.

I thank my late father, Tony R. Baugh, Sr., for his pushing me as an adolescent to read and study a dictionary and a thesaurus, not to mention most of the *Encyclopedia Britannica*. I don't know if you could see on the horizon what I would become, but you helped instill in me a love for words and for acquiring knowledge that has never left me. I hope this book makes you proud.

To the man I call Dad, who happens to also be my pastor, Dr. Kevin R. White of Covenant Fellowship Church: thank you for introducing me to the art of Black preaching and to the panoply of Black preachers. "A Theology of Rejoicing" is an ode to you.

To my Covenant Fellowship Church family: thank you for the testimony of your laughter, your faith, and your joy. For all the kind words spoken, for all the meals prepared, for all the hugs hugged, for all the prayers prayed—thank you.

Many thanks are extended to my mentor, James Henry Harris, PhD, who has helped guide me through academia and who has helped shape my understanding of Black consciousness. Your scholarship has been a light to me. I never shall forget when you conferenced with me after class that day in Kingsley Hall four years ago. Your words were an oasis in a dry place. Thank you for writing the foreword to my first book! I'm honored to be your student.

I also want to thank Nimi Wariboko, PhD, my thesis advisor at Boston University, for taking a chance on me and trusting my vision and voice when it seemed few others in the academy did. Your tireless and unshattered brilliance is an inspiration to so many.

To Rashad Jones, my brother and my friend: thank you for being the original conversation partner to what would become my first book! My brother, you have no idea how much those many, many late-night text message conversations and phone calls, when we would talk for hours about what it means to be Christian and Black and free, when you would just let me philosophize in your ear as the night forged on, meant/mean to me, and how fundamental all those talks were to refining my scholarship. I'll never forget it.

To my good friend Shaunesse' Jacobs: thank you for your copious and detailed notes upon reading my original manuscript. Your honesty is only matched by your generosity.

To my dear friend Mayrenes Figuereo-Nellum: thank you for always being there to talk to and for showing an early interest in this book.

I want to also thank William McDonald, PhD; David Schnasa Jacobsen, PhD; Claudette Woodhouse; Rev. William T. Powell; Pastor Tory Dillard; Celine López Mendez; and Sophia DeLeon for reading some of the essays that would be included in this collection, and for their encouragement—your belief in my writing was the confirmation I needed to keep striving towards having the works published.

To my writing partner, my dog, Blu—for the past eight years, I don't know on how many walks we went, how many miles we daily traversed in the seclusion of the solitary free air, so many parks, so many quiet moments when the wind spoke almost as loudly as your bark—after a squirrel here, after a Canada goose there. I do know that those moments of blissful quiescence allowed me the grace to slow down, to compose my thoughts, many of which are here on these pages. I'll always cherish those times, and I'll always be inspired by how each day for you seemed a new adventure worth living.

And last but certainly never least, I would like to thank my genesis, my mother, Dolores White—my first teacher, my first confidante, my first supporter, my first champion, my portal into this world and into the world to come—thank you for being the first person to tell me I could be a writer that day when I was in second grade and I was sitting at the kitchen table working on a paper about the life of Sacagawea, and you looked over my shoulder and enthusiastically complimented my use of a parenthetical phrase. It's the early encouragement that rings loudest in the ear, and I want you to know that I never forgot that. Thank you for keeping me with you in the schoolhouse when you were grading papers. Thank you for teaching me how to ride a bike. Thank you for praying for me in the midnight hour. It has made my days bright. I wish you all the happiness that life can bring;

you deserve it for all you have done for me. This book would not be possible without you; I would not be possible without you. And that's facts. I love you forever and always.

Likewise the Spirit also helpeth our infirmities: for we know not what we should pray for as we ought: but the Spirit itself maketh intercession for us with groanings which cannot be uttered.

—Rom 8:26 KJV

1.

Introduction

"It don't even slap."

John Lennon got shot and died.
Cam'ron got shot and drove to the hospital in a Lamborghini.
Not even a contest.
—DESUS NICE

How do we assign value? Why do we esteem those we do over others? What are the metrics and matrices of this esteem? Who is truly deserving of our adulation? Who is worthy of our praise?

On July 4, 2020, President Donald Trump gave a speech at Mount Rushmore in which he made the following statement:

> I am here as your President to proclaim before the country, and before the world, this monument will never be desecrated, these heroes will never be defaced, their legacy will never, ever be destroyed, their achievements will never be forgotten, and Mount Rushmore will stand forever as an eternal tribute to our forefathers and to our freedom. . . . In our schools, our newsrooms, even our corporate boardrooms, there is a new far-left fascism, that demands absolute allegiance. If you do not speak its language, perform its rituals, recite its mantras, and follow

its commandments, then you will be censored, banished, blacklisted, persecuted, and punished. It's not going to happen to us.[1]

This Mount Rushmore speech is ultimately meaningless pandering, political maneuvering. It holds no real significance. Trump said that he will make sure that Mount Rushmore as a monument will never be brought down. First of all, no president, in the history of this nation, has ever had the best interests of Black people at heart and in mind. But let's just go with the presidents depicted in the gargantuan pewter frieze known as Mount Rushmore:

George Washington never cared about Black people. He deigned to own people as property. He enslaved 123 Black people and stipulated in his will that upon his death (on my birthday, December 14, 1799) he would only free those he enslaved after his wife, Martha, died.[2] Note the ease with which white people can afford to act or not act on matters of race, how insulated they are from it, even though they are the ones who created race: if it was righteous for Washington to release those he enslaved from their forced servitude, why not just do it? Why provide that it could only be done once his wife died? Why free them at all? Is the institution of slavery wrong or not, Mr. President? But President Washington didn't care about Black people. He even put several of those he enslaved in a particularly precarious position by offering them a paltry sum in exchange for their teeth to cure his mouth (or the mouth of another white person) of its eroding dentition.[3] Which enslaved person, considered as pure objects for extrinsic use, could refuse such an offer?

Thomas Jefferson never cared about Black people. He exemplified the core tenor of the biblical verse "ever learning, and never able to come to the knowledge of the truth."[4] He was known to study fifteen hours a day at one point in his life, using the waxen figure of candlelight to forge his erudite venturing deep into the night.[5] Yet, for all his study, for all his thirsting for information, he still could never arrive at the truthful conclusion that Black people are fully human. In addition to being an inveterate enslaver, a mandarin of the institution of slavery, he believed that Black people were not even capable of love. This further mystifies his pedophilic relationship with one of his enslaved workers, Sally Hemings, with whom he began having sexual intercourse on a trip to Paris when she, the mixed-race sister of Jefferson's

---

1. Trump, "Remarks by President Trump."
2. "Ten Facts about Washington," para. 14.
3. "George Washington and Teeth."
4. 2 Tim 3:7 KJV.
5. Randolph, *Domestic Life of Thomas Jefferson*, 15.

recently dead wife Martha, was just fourteen years old.[6] This was rape, and that of the most sordid kind: because Jefferson's epistemological commitments were that Black people and their descendants were not capable of love, all he could have ever experienced with Hemings was her sheer objectification, believing as he did that she could never comprehend the throes of romance. Even if she had assented to his advances, how could a fourteen-year-old enslaved girl, an *ipso facto* thing, ever offer such an autonomous reaction under those auspices? Jefferson knew this, yet he lay with her, having no love for her, as to him she could have no love for him. And so it was that he did to her literally what he did to his 135 inherited enslaved socially, politically, and economically—he fucked her.

Theodore "Teddy" Roosevelt never cared about Black people. And this is the man that was to be the bastion of progressivism in America—the man who was indomitable, the man of great drive, spirit, dynamism, and zeal for public service, who was said never to walk but to bound wherever it was that he was headed, who devoted time and monies to the preservation of nature and wildlife, who cared about the working man and the poor, who had every opportunity on multiple political plateaus (member of the New York State Assembly, then minority leader of the New York State Assembly, then president of the New York City Board of Police Commissioners, then assistant secretary of the navy, then governor of New York, then vice president of the United States, then president of the United States, all in a period of just nineteen years)[7] to positively affect the lives of millions of Black people in America and simply chose not to. Roosevelt, in many ways, is representative of the "passive morality with which" American presidents have standoffishly dealt with their Black citizenry. He believed in the central tenets of the Declaration of Independence, that "all men are created equal," but offered no consequential plans to enfranchise the Black person in America, instead clinging to the notion that it was up to the white race to train the Black race, as though it were their ethical responsibility,[8] as though it were their burden. This listless gradualism was indicative of the same feckless behavior for which Roosevelt was known when it came to the matter of social equitability between Black and white people. When Booker T. Washington, one of the great Black leaders of all ages, came to dine with President Roosevelt (soon after his inauguration in 1901) and discuss matters of racism and Black empowerment, white Southerners who heard about the meeting were in a fit; consequently, Roosevelt never invited another Black person to the White

6. Gordon-Reed, *Thomas Jefferson and Sally Hemings*, 217.
7. Biography.com Editors, "Theodore Roosevelt," para. 5–8.
8. Glass, "Theodore Roosevelt Reviews Race Relations," para. 5.

House for the remainder of his two terms in office, caring infinitely more about what white people thought than what Black people needed.

Abraham Lincoln never cared about Black people. He thought that realizing racial equality in the United States was impractical.[9] What does practicality have to do with anything? If he believed that Black people and white people were equal, would the matter of the practicable nature of legislating such a reality be totally infeasible? Was it rather, then, a matter of it being unfeasible rather than sensible? If that is the case, the proposed lack of practicality of slavery is but a ground within which to hide Lincoln's apathy towards the matter of slavery, or to interfere with slavery in the states where it existed. In the dialectic between practicality and moral rightness, the outcome should always be that which does not result in people being enchained. But Lincoln did, on the matter of American chattel enslavement, once proclaim in a letter to his friend Joshua Speed in 1855 that he chose "to bite his lip and keep quiet."[10]

Some will read this and wonder, "What about the Emancipation Proclamation?" The main reason Lincoln "freed the slaves" with the Emancipation Proclamation is that he wanted the Civil War to end. There had been emancipation proclamations before the official statement became enacted on January 1, 1863. One of Lincoln's generals, John C. Frémont, had put Missouri (a Southern, Union-loyal state) under martial law, informing Confederate sympathizers that their properties would be taken and their enslaved would be freed (an emancipation proclamation). Consequently, he was accosted by Lincoln who fired him from his post.[11] Emancipation was a wartime measure applying strictly to those states in open rebellion against the Union. There were no targeted, direct, or specific policies developed by the Lincoln administration to free all four million enslaved, enfranchise them on a legislative and cultural level, and render reparations for their 250 years of forced toil, denouncing the institution on a federal plane. Rather, Lincoln, through moments of apathy (abolitionists like Frederick Douglass and Harriet Tubman should be credited with the eradication of slavery more than Lincoln should) and tacit politicking, simply went with the flow of the tide of gradualism to the signing of a document that hastened the end of the Civil War, leading to the beginning of another civil war still being fought on the streets today. But what did he care? It's not like the whip was on his back.

While I'm on one, Barack Obama never cared about Black people. While his presence in the White House marked a moment of exultant

9. "Lincoln on Slavery," II, 222.
10. "Lincoln on Slavery," II, 255–56.
11. Franklin, "How Abraham Lincoln Fired," para. 9.

cultural beatification for Black peoples around the world, President Obama, the nation's first Black president, who had a political rise even more meteoric than Theodore Roosevelt, did nothing specifically for Black people on an executive level. He claimed to be the catholic president, a president for all people, yet he enacted no policy that specifically targeted the especial plight of Black people in America. Instead, he, the winner of the 2009 Nobel Peace Prize, dropped 26,171 bombs during his last year in office, said nothing when 550 Palestinian infants were killed by US-supported Israeli planes in fifty days in Gaza,[12] and failed to address the political and economic morass adversely affecting Black life in America. Let us never forget that it was during the Obama administration's second term that the Black Lives Matter movement, a decentralized and democratized social justice organization devoted to bringing awareness to and routing racially motivated violence against Black people, emerged. A Black Lives Matter movement emerged during the second term of America's first Black president. Never forget.

Most recently, President Obama, during the promotional stomping for his new memoir *A Promised Land*, made some disparaging remarks about the language of the current cry of the progressive wing of the Democratic Party to "defund the police," asserting that if those in the party who have now appropriated thematically what prison abolitionists have been advocating for some time (that there should be abolition of the prison industrial complex and the current national model of policing which sustains it, and that the funds apportioned to overfunded[13] local police departments by municipal centers should be divested into more productive areas of community engagement that prevents crime at its root—affordable housing, equitable education, healthy food programs, art enrichment initiatives, etc.) would just rephrase their request that somehow those who viscerally support the police with impregnable fervor would be more inclined to consider it. Consideration is the basest response to injustice. Action is what is required. But the former president's unwarranted and privileged comment has buried in it an unexpected fortune: we seem to finally have a glimpse beneath the saccharin, smooth surface of his cool-ass smile and into the soul of a man who has made a career upholding the securities of the people least affected by

---

12. West, *Race Matters*, 20.

13. In Tidewater, Virginia, where I am from, police departments are overfunded, and community programs are underfunded as a rule. In Chesapeake, for example, a neighboring city of Portsmouth where I grew up, in the 2020–2021 city budget, the police department had an operating store of $62,575,218; community services programs had been apportioned only $2,483,673. Even the mosquito control department received more monies than community enrichment programs in Chesapeake, with $5,067,496.

police brutality, people who mainly are not Black. Obama, we were rooting for you. We were all rooting for you.

No president has ever had the *best* interests of Black people at heart and in mind.

Second of all, who cares about Mount Rushmore? It don't even slap. And the man who sculpted it, Gutzon Borglum (real name), a Ku Klux Klan member, who also had a part in planning the relief sculpting on the vaunted exterior of Stone Mountain, which is the largest Confederate monument in the world, didn't even finish the carving of each of the four presidents he chose for the Mount because he died, and his son, Lincoln, could not finish what he began (each president was to have been depicted waist deep as opposed to only their visage) due to the loss of governmental funding.

A flop.

Tear it down if you will; leave it up if you want.

But be clear: in giving this speech, Trump is pressing a nonissue, unserious for the masses of Black people, most of whom (so far as I can tell, though I don't presume to speak for Black people) really don't care if Mount Rushmore stands or not. He is purposely clouding the matter at hand—*that the Confederate monuments should be removed* and removed for obvious reasons.

In no other historical instance have the losers of a war been able to hold political sway.

But this is America.

Here, the *losers* of its only civil war, traitors all, white supremacist racists to the very core, have not only been permitted to fly their insignia high along federal highways, but their unheroically dead are immortalized and glorified through the construction of multifarious monuments purposively strewn across the United States, and this years after their humiliating defeat (in my home state of Virginia, there has been a Confederate monument erected as recently as *1999*, in Powhatan, the Powhatan Troop Confederate Memorial[14]),[15] these monuments, in essence, suggesting both a character of

---

14. "Confederate Monuments in Virginia."

15. In *Interpretation Theory*, Paul Ricœur theorizes that written language serves a different role than the locutionary, illocutionary, and perlocutionary functions of spoken language. He compares the written word to the Renaissance paintings of Jesus, Mary the mother of Jesus, the apostle Paul, the apostle John, and others. Those iconographies, he suggests, were not those people but a mythologized interpretation of those people, through that narrativization lifted to another register of meaning and significance. The painters, be they Da Vinci or Raphael, were looking back at Jesus and Paul through their mind's eye and offering their explanation of who those beings were to them, lifting them to a place of empyrean mythos. This for Ricœur is the functionality of the written word. If we look at monuments as the written word, according to Ricœur, as texts

heroism and victimhood, which is definitively narcissistic, in effect monumentalizing whiteness as white supremacy throughout generations.

But this is the president who supposedly cares about Black people, the president who cares so deeply about historically Black colleges and universities, the president who has "done more for Black people than any other president in history."[16] But these statements make him a hypocrite because he says that he supports HBCUs (historically black colleges and universities) yet is categorically opposed to tearing down Confederate monuments. And this is a highly inconsistent position to hold.

Every HBCU has a storied and fascinating history of how it was founded, like how Wilberforce University was founded during the period of Enslavement, and it is the first HBCU to be owned and run by Black people or how Howard University was begun at a meeting of missionaries of the First Congregational Society of Washington, D.C. in 1866, specifically to be a seminary for training Black preachers. One of these stories is near and dear to my heart because I spent three years earning a master's degree upon the grounds on which that story emerged, that is, Virginia Union University in Richmond, Virginia:

By all accounts, Robert Lumpkin was a cruel slaver known often to whip and brutalize enslaved Black people. He owned and operated what came to be called Lumpkin's Jail in the second largest slaving city in America, where the enslaved were made to wait until they were sold. A veritable dungeon, "a place of sighs" (as characterized by abolitionist James B. Simmons), where, according to the account of one enslaved man there, the enslaved were made to dwell in a room only six or eight feet square, this enslaved man being fettered with iron to the point that his feet began to swell enormously, the fetters preventing him from removing his clothing in the day or at night, being fed rotten meat in an increasingly dank room filled with vermin and insects. These were the conditions of Lumpkin's Jail that were sustained from its incipience in the 1830s until Richmond was liberated in 1865 following the Union Army's victory over the Confederate Army. And so it was that Robert Lumpkin immediately fled (dying soon after), and the fifty enslaved were free.

---

themselves, we can be reminded that the monuments of Confederate soldiers are not the soldiers; they are merely interpretations of the men they represent, lifted to a place of myth. Therefore, Confederate monuments came years later after the Civil War. Their artisans, looking to mythologize and valorize those people, adhering more to memory and interpretation (through a racist hermeneutic) than to factual history, sought to make their own iconography.

16. Porterfield, "Trump Claims," para. 1.

In 1866, Mary Lumpkin, ironically the Black widow of Robert Lumpkin (she herself a former enslaved person), with whom he fathered five daughters, became legal owner of the property of the now defunct Lumpkin's Jail; in 1867, Ms. Lumpkin sold all her late husband's property to a Minister Nathaniel Colver, Baptist. After pulling out the bars that gated many of the rooms in the edifice, Colver started a seminary for Black people on the grounds and in the building formerly known as Lumpkin's Jail (to educate some of the four million newly freed people). From this school, called Colver Institute (later called Richmond Theological Institute), in a small eventuation of time, came the unionizing of Wayland Seminary in Washington, D.C., and Richmond Theological Institute into what would be known as Virginia *Union* University since 1899.[17]

This history is relevant because it reveals that one cannot be against the removal of Confederate monuments, or monuments that valorize slaveholders for that matter, and be in favor of funding HBCUs. It is a matter of high ethical and rhetorical consistency. How so? Because there in Richmond, a former capital of the Confederate States of America, stood a jail that served to enslave those heroic humans, forcing them by means of brutality and callousness to suffer in the bleakest conditions in a purgatory of white supremacist design as they awaited a hellish fate—that they would be bought and sold into slavery, made to be nothing more than property. This jail was a monument to white supremacy, yet it was brought low and torn down to build a school—and not just any school—a school for Black people and the progeny of Black people so that they might be educated to enact their own social liberation and exaltation.

A monument was pulled down.

Today, there is a marvelous opportunity for the highest office of this land to stand in solidarity with the cry for justice from Black people by simply removing Confederate statues, which stand to venerate people who brutalized the ancestors of over forty million of its citizens, affirming an intimidating white supremacist configuration of governance in this nation in the process. There is an opportunity today, if Trump really cares about Black people, to, from the granite dust of freshly moved monuments, construct a landscape that uplifts Black people in a way similar to what VUU has done for thousands of students for the past 155 years. Virginia Union University could be a novel model for how futurity can be actualized through meaningful construction where there once stood monumental destitution.

Yet, for this president, it is a moment of contrived contention: it is a moment for self-aggrandizement, for grandstanding. Why? Because, though

---

17. This account was found in Tucker, "Digging up the Past."

he accuses the masses of Black people, and those who would ally themselves to our cause, of establishing some sort of ritualistic system of comportment, he is the very one who demands the fealty of empty words, rewards mindless sycophancy, and requisites activity that, through the performativity of acceptable actions, has the veneer of patriotism yet never actually holds the nation accountable for how it is still so very far from its lofty proposed ideals; he is the very one who demands certain behaviors from America's citizens (standing for the national anthem, saluting the American flag, remaining uncritical of the Founding Fathers, etc.), and those who oppose his jingoistic standard are labeled unpatriotic and un-American. This kind of thinking is neo-fascist to its core.[18]

And that is what this collection of essays, a mixtape of sorts, part memoir, part narrative nonfiction, part theological, part philosophical, wholly personal, wrought out of a fraught societal milieu in a moment pregnant with pain and possibility, proposes (if what follows has any truly monographic unity): that there is a set of ritualized practices in this country, which have been instituted as a means of social acceptance, *a religion of white supremacy*, and how it is that we may combat it through an existential resistance to the dangerous texts that support it in American society at large, hopefully leading to the possibility of the creation of justice in our midst.

---

18. In *Sublime Object of Ideology*, Slavoj Žižek defines *fascism* as "an ideology ... based upon a purely formal imperative: Obey, because you must! In other words, renounce enjoyment, sacrifice yourself and do not ask about the meaning of it—the value of the sacrifice lies in its very meaninglessness; true sacrifice is for its own end; you must find positive fulfilment in the sacrifice itself, not in its instrumental value: it is this renunciation, this giving up of enjoyment itself, which produces surplus-enjoyment," an ideology that "demands obedience and sacrifice for their own sake" (89–90). He also warns that we should beware over-rapid historicization and over-rapid universalization, which "produces a quasi-universal Image whose function is to make us blind to its historical, socio-symbolic determination" and "makes us blind to the real kernel which returns as the same through diverse historicizations/symbolizations" (51), to not consider that fascism has only one way of appearing, e.g., Benito Mussolini and 1930s Italy. Just because what we are experiencing right now with Trump is not exactly Mussolini, we should not be deceived into believing that it is not just as fascist.

2.

On a Summer Being Stolen

And where is the safest place when that place must be someplace other than in the body?

—Claudia Rankine, Citizen

When I was but eighteen, facial hair just starting to connect, vernal starlight new in my eyes, I had a summer stolen.

At the beginning of the season, not long after my first year of college waned to a close, my girlfriend at the time drove down to Portsmouth from Richmond to see me. We spent the whole day together, the taut Virginian humidity a sanguine spice in our noses, a flare reflective of the carefree passions of an inchoate love. Night was soon to arrive, the crepuscular hour was splayed on the horizon, when we drove to a secluded spot I knew, shielded from the oculus of I-264 oncoming traffic by trees and weeds and thick vegetation. We made clumsy, breathy love in her silver 2002 Honda Civic until the eventide bent more towards midnight, the stars above our lampshade.

I was on lookout, her back facing the nearby street that abutted a cul-de-sac. A car drove by. Nothing major. No need to stop. Another pair of headlights jammed the black of night away. It's nothing. Then another car drove by, the familiar mingled drone of engine sputter and valence, only this time, the side of the vehicle streamed red and white and blue, with "CHESAPEAKE POLICE" in red. I tell my girlfriend that I saw a cop and she immediately unstraddles me, pulls up her Guess jeans in the driver seat, knowing only with a telepathy informed by a legacy of inner-city overpolicing that the car, though passed, would for some reason return.

I knew too.

    I throw the condom out the window in the nearby woods. I do not know why I do this, but for some reason the act flows from my being with parasympathetic instinctiveness. Sure enough, the cop has turned around to investigate, the allure of a parked car on a public street with its headlights unlit apparently too much to pass up. He drives up to the car, gets out, shines his light in through the windows as he begins to knock, knock, knock. My girl lowers the window. "What're you doing out here?" he demands. "Nothing. Just sitting in the car," she responds. A lie. A good lie. A necessary lie. After all, what business of his was it what we were doing? We obviously weren't breaking any laws and we certainly did not present any clear danger to ourselves or to others. So, why the interrogation?

    Out of nowhere another patrol car pulls up to the scene of our crime of being two Black youths sitting in a car unbothered and bothering no one. Another car pulls up. Another car pulls up. Another car pulls up. Yet another car pulls up. All these police cruisers for two unarmed Black teens. By this time, it had been requested us by Officer Racially-Motivated-Supererogation that we step out of the car so that he and some of the ten other police officers present could search it. For what? We, being teenagers, so afraid of what would happen to us (I knew that we were in Chesapeake, a city known for police officers who were racist in their pursuit of Black people) if we put up any resistance at all. I am ashamed to say that I did not know my constitutional rights as an eighteen-year-old. This is ten years before the Ferguson saga would unfold, ten years before Tamir Rice was violently disallowed from playing with a toy gun, eight years before a crazed white vigilante sought an airy word of vengeance with a Black boy, who just wanted to enjoy his sugary concessions on a walk home. The public consciousness was not toward Black life mattering then (as it really has never been). I did not know that, according to the Fourth Amendment, I could not be searched without just cause or that, according to the landmark 1968 case *Terry v. Ohio*, the only way I could be searched is if it could be proved without a shadow of doubt that I endangered life.[1] But we were young, vulnerable, scared citizens, who were having a night that we would never forget, for the wrong reasons.

    After these unfortunate people searched the car, two of them stepped forward in the blare of the halogen lights of their patrol units to search my girlfriend and me, while the other eight of them stared on with snarky, satisfied grins. We were searched with simultaneity, a white male officer frisking my being, while a white female officer groped the girl I loved. This is an

---

1. Alexander, *New Jim Crow*, 63.

important detail because she did not frisk her, but she fondled her as the male officers looked on intently. The male officer who frisked me then said some intimidating words to me about not being where I should and so forth and so on, saying something of a soliloquy to one of his fellow officers about cameras being in the trees (?), how they may have been recording us. Then, he gave us our driver's licenses back, and sent us on our way, disheveled, disabused, and dishonored.

On the way back to my house (where else would we go after such an emaciating encounter), which was only three minutes away from where we were, my girlfriend broke the stark silence of a night that had begun so harmlessly and said that she felt violated. And in that moment, I felt a sense of powerlessness that I had never before known—that I had no control over the situation, that I could not even protect the girl that I loved. I had to just sit there and take it. We both did.

I look back on that experience from my youth now as a grown man, when my summer was stolen (because after that, which was such a caustic occurrence, all other red-letter events that season were dulled in comparison), and two things are inimitably clear to me: 1) I remember immediately after, as we drove back to my house, feeling guilty for what had happened, feeling as though that unspeakable event were my fault, feeling that I deserved to experience that because I was having pre-marital sex, which reveals the insufficiency of rote, unthought theologies presented to young people in our churches from a young age. 2) I am instantly reminded of the words of Ta-Nehisi Coates, how he defines racism in his book *Between the World and Me* as "the need to ascribe bone-deep features to people and then humiliate, reduce, and destroy them."[2] And in that moment, that moment now so long ago, a moment ensconced in a time of implacable delight, a season of romance that was sure to be ours, though I did not feel destroyed, I was, we were, utterly humiliated and reduced, and for no other reason than that we were Black.

---

2. Coates, *Between the World and Me*, 6.

3.

Preaching and Justice

The Hermeneutics of Liberation and Resistance

Marx's dictum is, "The ideas of the dominant class become the dominant ideas." Marx, moreover, understood well that in the end, the dominant class does not need to exercise force but holds sway by "hegemonic theatre."
—Walter Brueggemann, Word Militant

According to William Dilthey, hermeneutics as the "art of understanding expressions of life fixed in writing" always draws attention to itself only "during a great historical movement."
—Rudolf Bultmann, New Testament and Mythology

You can only be destroyed by believing that you really are what the white world calls a nigger. I tell you this because I love you, and please don't you ever forget it.
—James Baldwin, "My Dungeon Shook: Letter to My Nephew on the Hundredth Anniversary of the Emancipation" in Fire Next Time

I feel like my entire life has been a protest.

—VIOLA DAVIS[1]

Thomas Jefferson, celebrated third president of the United States, thoughtful composer of the Declaration of Independence, erudite Founding Father of America, believed that Africans and the descendants of Africans were subhuman, a point he made clear in his seminal *Notes on the State of Virginia*, in which he used racially exclusionary rhetoric to advocate for the establishment of a colony in Africa (that would become Liberia), not on the basis of reuniting the progeny of Africans with their motherland, but that of his feeling that they should not be integrated with white people due to their inferiority. He was greatly influenced by Immanuel Kant in this philosophy, whose *Observations on the Feeling of the Beautiful and Sublime* became a bulwark of racial primacy and prosperity for the descendants of Europeans during the so-called Age of Enlightenment. In 1763, some thirteen years before Jefferson would begin the work of composing the Declaration of Independence, Kant, his philosophical paragon, writes:

> The Negroes of Africa have by nature no feeling that rises above the trifling. Mr. Hume challenges anyone to cite a single example in which a Negro has shown talents, and asserts that among the hundreds of thousands of blacks who are transported elsewhere from their countries, although many of them have even been set free, still not a single one was ever found who presented anything great in art or science or any other praiseworthy quality, even though among the whites some continually rise aloft from the lowest rabble, and through superior gifts earn respect in the world. So fundamental is the difference between these two races of man, and it appears to be as great in regard to mental capacities as in color. The religion of fetishes so wide spread among them is perhaps a sort of idolatry that sinks as deeply into the trifling as appears to be possible to human nature. A bird feather, a cow's horn, a conch shell, or any other common object, as soon as it becomes consecrated by a few words it is an object of veneration and invocation in swearing oaths. The blacks are very vain but in the Negro's way, and so talkative that they must be driven apart from each other with thrashing.[2]

This ridiculously presumptuous, unhinged, and unwarranted siege of African ontology being obviously problematic on its own, what is apparent

---

1. Saraiya, "Viola Davis," para. 5.
2. Kant, *Observations*, 110–11.

here is a constitutive epistemological framework that was so provocative in its time that it pierced the imagination and phenomenology of an entire generation of thinkers, who were not living in a "textless world," who were "[abiding] by texts known and unknown."[3] Jefferson and the other Founding Fathers were creating a new world by and through text, a "scripting tradition of the Enlightenment [exercising] an incredible pervasive hegemony,"[4] a world that disclaimed and discounted the very existence of Black peoples, who would be *unable to inhabit it*. It was in this way that Jefferson began the highly textual work of actualizing the ideal democracy that he had conceptualized, in the "dominant scripting of reality . . . rooted in the Enlightenment enterprise associated with Descartes, Locke, Hobbes, and Rousseau,"[5] which did not have in mind African peoples and their descendants. Concordantly, Paul Ricœur posits:

> To explain a text then means primarily to consider it as the expression of certain socio-cultural needs and as a response to certain perplexities well localized in space and time.[6]

Because of this textual reality, in the United States, there will always exist the specter of a brutally racist past. This is no truer than in the languages that are used to evince a certain awareness of surroundings. For what is more ubiquitous than language? Consequently, it is imperative that the matter of language, those narrativized realms created by human minds, be metered and conducive to the production of a viable, human ecology, one that is not exclusive and delimiting but inclusive and pluralistic. Language, like Black theology, and any good theology of preaching, should always be for the purposes of beatification and liberation. Therefore, this essay shall explore the ways in which the bold ontological experience of the Black person in America can serve as a model hermeneutic posture (perspective of interpretation) that immanently generates a theology of reaching liberation through a theoretical transference (influence) of consciousness from the lived Black experience to the benthos of the white psychical experience.

I once read an article in *The Wall Street Journal* about a group of working-class Congolese men, "taxi drivers, carpenters, [and] gravediggers," called *Sapeurs*, who spend much of their income on dressing well because, in doing so, they feel a sense of redemption, exaltation, and beatification."[7]

---

3. Brueggemann, *Word Militant*, 23.
4. Brueggemann, *Word Militant*, 24.
5. Brueggemann, *Word Militant*, 24.
6. Ricœur, *Interpretation Theory*, 90.
7. Downey, "Beau Brummels of Brazzaville," para. 1.

I thought about this article and wondered if this kind of beatification had been extended to a larger group of people, a demographic, namely the African American race. For, if there's any race of peoples in need of beatification, it is the so-called African American race. More than any other in America, more than any race in the history of race, the Black person in America has been viciously brutalized in the cruelly real demonstrations of man's inhumanity to man: historically, they have been pillaged, waylaid, with their places of residence utterly destroyed. They were brought up from the tenably ingenuous, ingenious glory they had in their forms of civilized society and made as nothing in the face of Germanic grimaces and smiles alike: disenfranchised, discredited, disannulled, dismayed, and disintegrated from all they ever knew, they were brought out of their reality into another's and forced to conform to a European archetypal ideal. Therefore, the African American people were indeed direly in need of the salvific sartorial cloak of social justice through languaging, namely through an ontology of textual resistance,[8] a hermeneutic posture that they have cultivated and continue to maintain, evidenced in a perennial resistance. This resistance, this fugitivity, is regarding *text*, and it is as Henry Louis Gates Jr. hypothesizes, "resistance to white supremacy [that] never ceased among African Americans, despite the unbearably hostile climate that white supremacy created, as it morphed from the justification of slavery into ever more repulsive forms in response to slavery's abolition and the onset of Reconstruction."[9]

When I was a boy, we would often travel from Ettrick, Virginia (where I lived at the time), about forty minutes northward, about fifteen minutes outside of Richmond (where I was born), to an amusement park called King's Dominion. Through an act of filial transmission of personal cultural preference, my father's favorite rollercoaster became my favorite rollercoaster. This coaster in question was unique to the park, not so much in its construction (it was and still is a basic metal, bar-fastened car affixed upon

---

8. This idea of resistance was influenced by Angela D. Sims's essay "Re-Orientation" from the book *Womanist Theological Ethics*, in which she examines how "power dynamics can shape cultural values" (259) by cognitively reorienting how we view lynching as exemplification of the oppressor/oppressed dichotomy and how a naming of the injustices wrought by this power dynamic can lead to the actuation of justice. According to Sims, there needs to be a reframing, a reimagining, a reengaging with how oppressed peoples have been articulated historically and contemporaneously; that the purpose of reorientation is not only to display the ways in which God reveals God-self in all people but also "to debunk truth misrepresentations that promote the suppression of other expressions of reality" (263). In this way, reorientation is a form of resistance that seeks to shift the culpability of oppression from the routinized and systematic degradation of the oppressed, societally disparaged, to those in positions of power.

9. Gates, *Stony the Road*, 131.

a wood-lined railway, after the aboriginal concepts and style of a Black man, Granville T. Woods, who invented a similar rollercoaster in 1909) but in its execution. This ride had two sides—one that went traditionally forwards, and one that went ironically backwards—a *rebellion*. My father enjoyed the backwards side, and so I did too. The name of this rollercoaster was (and still is) "The Rebel Yell."

This is Virginia. It is a state whose vexillological and thus political commitments are to never tolerate the domination of tyrants (*Sic semper tyrannis*), yet it is a commonwealth that valorizes the invidious legacies of its white supremacist ancestry and Confederate statehood, even on the level of children's entertainment. That both my father and I came of age going to this very theme park that had as one of its main attractions a ride named after the battle cry of a defeated and traitorous white supremacist nation state, and that we used to take part in enjoying its high velocity twists and turns, hands held high, bursting smiles beaming joys, sheds light on just how inured we had become to the commonplaceness of it all: the incalculable ills of white supremacy had at once psychologically hardened us and become utterly meaningless to us with seeming simultaneity. Its fabric so deeply woven, so trenchantly dedicated to memorializing its fictive greatness that even amusement becomes the site of horror and thus the site of resistance. Note the concurrent tragedy and triumph, how Black people in America must live through times of turmoil to live bountifully into visions of victory. When I think back on that time, ten years younger now than my father would ever live to be, I realize the jubilant shout that echoed from the rollercoaster was actually a groan in the throat.

When I was a boy, my father compelled me to study both the dictionary and the thesaurus. I already had an affinity for language, but I immediately developed a love of words—specific words, incisive words, bleating words. They filled me with a dynamism that I had not previously known. Admittedly, I began this lexicographical quest partly with a juvenile goal in mind—to impress my friends: I would learn these words to heighten my "Yo mama" joking ability. I already had a facility for constructing a deft "Yo mama" joke, especially one relative, for some reason, to a corpulent mother: "Yo mama so fat she has to iron her clothes in a parking lot." "Yo mama so fat she got baptized at Sea World." "Yo mama so fat she bent over to pick up a dollar and caused an eclipse." "Yo mama so fat she got hit by a bus and said, 'Who hit me with that rock?'" "Yo mama so fat she sat on a quarter and squeezed a booger out of George Washington's nose." I was *pretty* good. So, when I learned the word *hebetudinous*, I thought, "Wow. That's a good one." Now was the time to diversify my "Yo mama" repertoire to include jokes about my opponent's matriarch's dearth of intelligence. And so, I began to learn every synonym for *stupid* I could: doltish, sophomoric, dull, dimwitted, puerile, hebetudinous, with hebetudinous being the clear favorite of the bunch. He-be-tu-di-nous. It was such a phonically pleasing word. Perhaps it was its bawdy multisyllabic construction. Maybe it was the way it seemed to lilt itself mellifluously from the page. Or maybe it was the innate logics of its movement from consonantal accidents, from the *h* to the *b* to *t* to the *d*. Gorgeous. The word seemed so complete in itself, and I wished deep within that I were as complete within myself as it was. Nevertheless, it was then that I immediately incorporated it into my new "Yo mama" jokes, much to the chortling delight of my friends.

When I became a man, putting away childish things (linguistically and otherwise), as they were, I began to deepen my study of the American Standard English and British Standard English lexicons, and I learned about the terms that were used—apportioned to refer to my ancestors, those piteous, remarkable, wretched saints—terms devised by those who later would be characterized as pseudoscientists. These terms were devised by white men like Samuel A. Cartwright, who in 1851, created words like *dysaesthesia Æthiopica* (*n*. also called *rascality*, the dullness of the Negro causing an inability of the Negro to feel pain or pleasure)[10] and *drapetomania* (*n*. the tendency of the Negro to run away from his state of enslavement), the former term using the word root of my precious *hebetudinous* to constitute its

---

10. The textuality of this belief of the insensitivity of Black people's nervous system was also believed to be in part due to the perception that Black people had thicker skin than white people, an ideology that pervaded American consciousness long after Emancipation. Black people were in some cases commoditized on multiple levels in American life, as in the case of, upon their death, being made into shoes. An account of this unbelievable practice appeared in the Philadelphia newspaper *The Mercury* on Saturday, March 17, 1888 (as disclosed in the Ferris State University Jim Crow Museum of Racist Memorabilia in an April 2013 article entitled *Human Leather*), in which a journalist gives an account of a local doctor he met and his curious footwear: "'Is the down trodden African still beneath your feet?' In the most matter of fact way, and without the shadow of a smile, he answered: 'I suppose you mean to inquire if I still wear shoes made of the skin of a negro. I certainly do, and I don't propose changing in that respect until I find a leather that is softer and will last longer and present a better appearance.' ... The doctor's shoes always exhibit a peculiarly rich lustrousness in their blackness. He assures me that they never hurt his feet. The new pair he was using when I last saw him emitted no creaking sound and appeared as comfortable as though they had been worn a month. Their predecessors, he told me, had been in constant use for eight months. He obtains the skins from the bodies of negroes which have been dissected in one of our big medical colleges. The best leather is obtained from the thighs. The soles are formed by placing several layers of leather together. The skin is prepared by a tanner at Womseldorf, 16 miles from Reading. The shoes are fashioned by a French shoemaker of this city, who knows nothing of the true character of the leather, but who often wonders at its exquisite smoothness, and says that it excels the finest French calf-skin."

meaning, further saying that it is consequent of the Negro having "so great a *hebetude* of the intellectual faculties, as to be like a person half asleep."[11] At that moment, at that hour, I stopped using the word hebetudinous; that which had been a friend to me had become my enemy. Reading the description of Cartwright's use of the word still haunts me.

I suppose we are all at the mercy of ghosts of some kind. Memories from a distant past are still present with us. But the ghosts of the Black person are etched into the language, the phraseologies upon which the very nation hoists its blood-striped vexillology, its flag. And this is the problem. Unlike her white counterpart, the Black person today must deal with the lexilogical mischief of the past, in the form of words printed on the page, in the form of Confederate monuments, in the form of the very currency used to eke out a living (President Andrew Jackson, who is on the twenty-dollar bill, was a most brutal enslaver. He would often take out ads in local newspapers querulously advocating for the return of runaway enslaved persons to be returned to him, sometimes upping the price of the bounty if they were tortured first, like this one from 1804:

> Stop the Runaway.
> FIFTY DOLLARS REWARD.
> ELOPED from the subscriber, living near Nashville, on the 25th of June last, a Mulatto Man Slave, about thirty years old, six feet and an inch high, stout made and active, talks sensible, stoops in his walk, and has a remarkable large foot, broad across the root of the toes—will pass for a free man, as I am informed he has obtained some means, certificates as such—took with him a drab great-coat, dark mixed body coat, a ruffled shirt, cotton homespun shirts and overalls. He will make for Detroit, through the states of Kentucky and Ohio, or the upper part of Louisiana. The above reward will be given any person that will take him, and deliver him to me, or secure him in jail, so that I can get him. If taken out of the state, the above reward, and all reasonable expences paid—and ten dollars extra, for every hundred lashes any person will give him, to the amount of three hundred.
> ANDREW JACKSON
> Near Nashville, State of Tennessee[12])

in the form of unspoken normatives once overtly shared that pervade the ideologies of the political divide, in the form of housing districts redlined, in the form of the emendations to the "Star-Spangled Banner" and the

---

11. Cartwright, "Report on the Diseases." Italics added.
12. Brown, "Hunting Down Runaway Slaves," para. 1.

Constitution and the Declaration of Independence, their original, and indeed only intent to nullify *her* freedoms and *her* liberties and *her* pursuit of happiness in a milieu of estrangement. She is suffocated by the weight of texts that work against her in the present, and she is accosted by texts that haunt her from the past, "texts and monuments [that have been] understood in different ways . . . as sources for reconstructing a picture of some past age or period of time."[13]

Consequently, that social justice does not seem to be on the horizon for the Black person, there tends to be engendered in her a rigidity not to yield, to suffer any form of oppression. This is the lacuna of her resistance. The Black person seeks to disarm and inoculate all weapons of oppression, even down the phonemes of lexicography that pervade the structures of the societal and governmental design of the nation she inhabits. All forms of oppression are being annulled. This is the only justifiable explanation for the constant use of the racial epithet "n—," a term that for centuries had been apportioned for the Black person to immure and dehumanize her, modifying it to the word, "nigga." Today, the Black person is finished with all forms of oppression. Nevertheless, the Black person needs beatification. Thus, there is no sense in her bowing her energies, her dynamism of self to the nether regions of impropriety and debasement, but rather to sanctify herself with all forms galvanic to constructing her person, including the disarmament of all forms of oppression. To disarm all weapons of oppression, even those extant in language, is an ambition of the Black person in the twenty-first century. She says *nigga* as a term applicable to her particulars, her friends, in part to reveal the absurdity of the term (a n— has only ever existed in the minds of white people), and in hopes that it will soon become innocuous and thus its patho-lexicology be tranquilized. Moreover, the Black person seeks to disarm and inoculate all weapons of bigotry and racism, which have been directed at her so often and with such inevitable eventuation, even down to the phonemes of lexicography that pervade the substructures of the societal design of America.

In his great book, *Stony the Road: Reconstruction, White Supremacy, and the Rise of Jim Crow*, Henry Louis Gates Jr. describes the ways in which whenever some strides are made to enfranchise Black people on the margins of society, there is a disruption within the white populace, the dominant class, to repress it. He connects the legislative precedents of litigious incidents that worked to integrate and socialize formerly enslaved people of African descent into America following the Civil War, from Reconstruction in favor of redeeming the humanity of Black people, to Redemption, which

---

13. Bultmann, *New Testament and Mythology*, 79.

was a response by white racists to undermine such societal, economic, and political advancements. What makes this text fascinating is not just in Gates Jr.'s staggering historical excavation of a meticulously mounted white supremacist assault on the political, economic, and cultural lives of African Americans post-Civil War, a movement called the Lost Cause (which led to the construction of Confederate Monuments across the United States), supposed white superiority systemically pervades the very substructures of American society, even unto this good day. He writes, with particular focus on white supremacist ideology evidenced as Black stereotyping:

> Stereotypes of Black people within each of these discourses interpenetrated each other, as it were. Nineteenth-century racial science reflected characterizations of Black people inherited from eighteenth-century natural philosophy, such as racist speculations by David Hume and Immanuel Kant and Thomas Jefferson. Social science reinforced observations about Black people's habits and character from travel accounts and individuals' journals. Zoologists or natural historians such as Louis Agassiz used the emerging art of photography as visual proof of dubious theories of the evolution of human beings. Legal opinions grounded their reasoning in the irrefutability of what we now can see were the commonplaces of scientific racism. The Negro's image was trapped in a viciously claustrophobic circle, and so, therefore, were actual Negroes, the freedmen and freedwomen so recently liberated from inherited bondage.[14]

He continues:

> By the 1890s—precisely when Jim Crow was hardening—one of the most popular means of advertising products to American consumers was to juxtapose the product or its virtues with supremely demeaning images of African Americans. So popular were they with the public, so widespread was their utilization, in the South, in North, and beyond the nation's borders, that virtually anywhere a white person saw an image of an African American, she or he was encoded in one of these stereotypes as somehow laughably ignorant, subhuman, devoid of thought and reason, ruled by one's senses, as would be an animal.... In other words, when a white person confronted an actual Black human being, he or she was "already a text," to use Barbara Jordan's insightful definition of stereotype. It didn't matter what the individual Black man or woman said and did, how much education he or she had, or whether they were from the North or the

---

14. Gates, *Stony the Road*, 131.

South, because negative images of them in popular imagination already existed, and were already *fixed*, imposed upon them like hoods or masks. This practice of xenophobic masking, as it were, *still exists*.[15]

If it is so that the Black human is "already a text," it, the life of the Black person, therefore, must be a form of textual resistance against those texts that would seek to annihilate her. Thus, it, the life of the Black person, is not a life subjected to the inherent textness of the world around it, as Walter Brueggemann writes, needful of the ways in which the written word becomes commensurate with applicable truths or tautologies. Rather, instead of passively participating in the being of language,[16] its vivified corpus pervading the atmosphere of vaunted, lofty ideas, the Black person as a being *actively participates in her irreplaceableness* by repurposing old languages and generating new languages that affirm her. Since theology begins in the body, the Black person has consequently embodied a theology of resistance that has been innately stipulating the Ricœurian concept that "the sense of the text is in front of it."[17] *The sense of the text is in front of it*. Therefore, making use of the eternal interplay of opposites,[18] it could be asserted in the inverse that because the sense of the text is in front of it that the insensateness of the text is behind it. To be insensate is to be dead. Thus, if the sense of the text is in front of it, the life also of the text is in front of it. For the Black person, getting in front of the text, where the text lives and moves and has its being, where the text is actualized and realized, is not actually voluntary—it is a mode of survival. How can the Black person be expected to live a full and robust life, when with constant bombardment, she is oft affronted with languages and phraseologies and narratives that are seldom redemptive and reductionist? How can she be expected to ever live a fulfilled existence? She must, therefore, not only get in front of the text, she must live a life that is constantly *in front of the text,* because in front of the text there is life, in front of the text she may run in and out and find pasture for her soul.

Behind the text there is death, not only because the author is dead (Roland Barthes, *The Death of the Author*) but because the words written about her are deadening, deathly, and deleterious. Behind the text is Kant, behind the text is Hume, behind the text is Jefferson, behind the text is Wilson,

---

15. Gates, *Stony the Road*, 131.
16. Bakhtin, *Toward a Philosophy*, 41.
17. Ricœur, *Interpretation Theory*, 87.
18. Jacques Derrida, as discussed by Nicholas Royle in his book *Jacques Derrida*, has a concept called différance, in which Derrida reveals meaning through opposites as a mode of textual deconstruction.

behind the text is Nixon, behind the text is Trump—in front of the text is a world perennially unexplored, whose possibility towards the extirpation of injustice is ever-imminent, and the potential for justice is endless. The Black person is thus a novel and ingenious interlocutor with the textuality of the logocentric universe. Her requisite and rampant challenging of lexicology, liberative and beatifying for the forgotten among her, is instructive. Now, when there is talk of an election being stolen, when the very fabric of American democracy is unraveling before our eyes, what now could be more relevant than taking a hermeneutic posture that instantly resists the cultural and symbolic hegemony, such as presidential lies and the mendacity that so oozes from the White House?

Theologically, it is necessary to assume a position ontologically that requisites existing protextually, in front, even beyond the text, as it were. This is like what James Henry Harris, in his book, *Preaching Liberation*, considers:

> The first questions the preacher may ask are, What does this high sounding word have to do with the liberation struggle? Why should Black preachers be concerned about *hermeneutikos*? The answer lies in the fact that preachers are compelled to interpret Scripture and convey their meaning to the people in the pews . . . . However, the few who have acknowledged the importance of an inclusive and pluralistic approach to interpreting history and the Bible have been Black preachers and theologians, feminist and womanist theologians, and the Latin American liberation preachers and teachers . . . . In liberation hermeneutics, meaning is based on one's perception of social struggle as well as the reality of the social, political, and religious ecology. Therefore, Black folks' interpretation of the Bible and their environment is not based on Hegel's historicity or Max Weber's analysis of the social setting, but rather an understanding of their own experience and history.[19]

With that in mind, it can clearly be seen that before there can be a liberation homiletics, there must first be a liberation hermeneutics, steeped in one's own context and one's own orientation to the plight of the oppressed. The context in this instance is that of Black people in America, and this can also be the site of justice, the decentered self learning from the Black experience of textual resistance.

In *The Word Militant*, Brueggemann explains how there are no "textless worlds," but everything in the universe that we occupy is influenced by

---

19. Harris, *Preaching Liberation*, 59–60.

text and is rife with textuality, being subordinate to text, that "reality itself is scripted, that is, shaped and authorized by the text."[20] With a similar reverence for the logocentricity of the world, Paul Ricœur in his *Interpretation Theory: Discourse and the Surplus of Meaning* discloses, again, that the sense of the text is in front of it. Remember, it could be construed that what is behind the text is meaninglessness configured as death—death of imagination, death of intent, death of meaning:

> Taking the notion of depth semantics as our guideline, we can now return to our initial problem of the reference of the text. We can now give a name to this non-ostensive reference. It is the kind of world opened up by the depth semantics of the text, a discovery, which has immense consequences regarding what is usually called the sense of the text. The sense of a text is not behind the text, but in front of it. It is not something hidden, but something disclosed. What has to be understood is not the initial situation of discourse, but what points towards a possible world.[21]

Each and every interpretation begins with the sense of a text (a *guess*), which is foundational to moving to a place of reference (understood here as *understanding*). Thus, the sense of a text must not be befuddled by the death note pastness of it but must be lucidly free of all hampering, destructive intent that could inhibit how it can shape the formation of a more equitable future. Therefore, briefly using Brueggemann for description, Ricœur for prescription, and Harris for inspiration, I want to establish a theology of preaching that does not merely rely on a hermeneutic posture that is in front of the text, but to generate an ontology that learns from the experience of Black people in America, a land that stipulates it.

For Black people, textuality in the Western tradition has never been a benefit. Indeed, the United States was founded upon a textuality that intended to obviate their very being. Again, I am thinking here particularly of the Declaration of Independence, inspired by Enlightenment period writings (especially Kant's *Observations on the Feeling of the Beautiful and Sublime*), which specifically enumerated the ways in which people of African ancestry were inferior to people of European ancestry. These are the very texts that constituted and constitute (the present tense is very important here) the very nation in which Black people live. Thus, Black people have had to construct a mode of being that is always pre-textual, that always lives in front of the text because to live behind the text or even *in it* means certain death.

20. Brueggemann, *Word Militant*, 23.
21. Ricœur, *Interpretation Theory*, 87.

This is certainly a twenty-first-century hermeneutic, one that lives into an existentialism of resistance to normatives of hierarchy, hegemonic powers, and functional anti-relationality (animated by an adherence to the textuality of a logocentric universe, expressed, in this case, as American society). It is resistance as lifestyle, of living as act of reframing, refurbishing, and redesigning modalities of explanation of self. It is the living reality of text resistant to text, not allowing appropriation in the Ricœurian sense, that is, the textual imparting of a new self into our egos; but it is a sense of the text that is habitually and naturally in motion towards its incisive reference—a freer future. This seamless movement from sense to reference can only take place in the life of a hermeneutic that redounds to an acceptance of an ever-redemptive narrative of one's own irreplaceability.

Remember, this is an approach that is to have a two-pronged response. First, there is the work of liberation. This begins in the act of adopting and adapting an ontological hermeneutic reflective of the naturally inhabited, courageous historical epistemic resistance of Black life. Second, there is to be the work of beatification, that is, the reframing of texts to dialectically confront destructive texts to create what is an emergently more generative and productive *word* for the oppressed interlocutor with the text. How we locate this *word* in our cultural context will look differently in different social arenas. It may be that the resister is looking to remove Confederate monuments, or to change the name of military bases from those who chose domination and subjugation of human beings to the names of more redeemable personalities, or to finally perform the work of issuing reparations for the four hundred years of systematic and systemic oppression of Black people in America. This is a work that is mobilized by an understanding of the ways in which texts in their multifarious forms invade our realities and administer their opinions of us; and how from thence we can either choose to uphold their decided sense of hegemony and dominion or resist their intention altogether, and how that resistance might resemble the light of justice. One does not have to be a preacher to adopt and adapt this hermeneutic methodology into one's own life and make it useful to the pulling down of strongholds, razing their very foundations. This is a work that seeks to first alter the terms of how text is understood, and then introduce a new understanding of text and hermeneutics to the formation to text as such, where there needs to be the intrusion of new redeeming texts. On this wise, Brueggemann writes:

> That text may be recognized or invisible. It may be a great religious classic or a powerful philosophical tradition or a long-standing tribal conviction. It is an account of reality that the

community comes to trust and to take for granted as a given that tends to be beyond reexamination. This text describes reality in a certain way and shape. In a world where there is more than one text, that is, a world of plurality, a given text may describe, but if another text intrudes, it is possible for that text to redescribe reality.[22]

Consequently, imagine a world in which Black people (like many of their white counterparts) ever considered David Hume a bastion of moral philosophy. Such a world would *never* exist. For if Black people ever accepted the textual reality of a Kant, they would no doubt not be able to live into an amenable and life-giving version of themselves. What is more, the Black person would be beholden and caged by the utter limitations of a text that proscribed their existential disparagement, with particular attention given to their dearth of artistic creativity; thus, the Black person would not be able to live into the possibility of further, anachronistic texts. For example, in *Observations*, Kant explicitly contends that peoples of African ancestry were/are incapable of creating great and meaningful art. If a Black person were to live under the pernicious weight and detrimental auspices of that text instead of in front of that text where there is life, where she may run in and out and find pasture of possibility, she would not be able to live into what Albert Camus would write years later that in order to evade, elide, and elude suicide (both physical and philosophical), one must create great art works best, assuaging the absurdity of life. If the Black person lives her life in or behind the Kant text as opposed to in front of it where Camus's *The Myth of Sisyphus* is (and beyond), how could she ever benefit from that wisdom, since she is not even capable of creating great art in the first place? She would be, in effect and in substance, occluded, precluded, and obviated from having a full and vigorous and robust life because of that proscription. Therefore, it has become the life praxis of the Black person to live with a hermeneutic posture that is ever-empowering, ever-uplifting, ever-beatifying, and ever-liberating.

In my essay "White Supremacy Is a Religion," I present a trichotomy of signs in the Peircean semiological tradition (icon→index→symbol) to point to the ways in which the African American is not a citizen in the very country that she built from the ground up *for free*. There, I critique the thought of Elisabeth T. Vasko, how she extends her theorization, apropos of dismantling the oppression of marginalized American citizenry, moving from her concept of "attentive listening" to introducing the concept of "sin-talk." She posits:

---

22. Brueggemann, *Word Militant*, 23.

> Sin-talk is what allows us to adequately describe and critique violence, terrorism, economic and racial inequality, and sexual exploitation. The metaphors we use to describe sin not only help us to name the ways in which we have been harmed, but they are also important in diagnosing our participation in the suffering of others.[23]

The problem here is that, though sincere in its theorization, it expresses naiveté and is utterly toothless in its actualization, particularly if America is personalized not as an agglomeration of peoples but as a *person*. As a person, who could ever convince America of sin? Who has ever been successful in compelling his conception that he indeed needs a savior? There have been those who have tried and who have been casualties of their prophetic outcry, either by exclusion, exile, or execution—people like Ella Baker, Marcus Garvey, Martin Luther King Jr., el-Hajj Malik el-Shabazz (Malcolm X), Fred Hampton, and Assata Shakur. Frederick Douglass thematized America's destructive personhood one summer in Rochester, New York, to no avail, when, in 1852, he fearlessly rendered his speech "What, to the Slave, is the Fourth of July?" in front of a predominantly white audience before whom he underscored the cognitive sickness of America's founders' desire to be free from the British, even fighting to secure that freedom through war, yet enslaving his people who wished for the same freedom from their oppressors. The peroration of this speech is one of the most scathing indictments on the discord in America's subjectivity and personhood ever recorded:

> Go where you may, search where you will, roam through all the monarchies and despotisms of the old world, travel through South America, search out every abuse, and when you have found the last, lay your facts by the side of the everyday practices of this nation, and you will say with me, that, for revolting barbarity and shameless hypocrisy, America reigns without a rival.[24]

This speech was given some eleven years before Emancipation (thirteen years before all the enslaved would be free), yet what Douglass said about America could still be asserted today without irony. Here, I would like to offer another trichotomy of signs, this time in hopes of revealing the desperate need for textual resistance, highlighting some of the more pernicious forms of texts appearing this hour. The obverse semiotics of citizenship for the Black person would be the semiotics of white citizenship in America, and upon what this citizenship might reckon for maintaining its foundation. In

---

23. Vasko, *Beyond Apathy*, 83.
24. Douglass, "What, to the Slave, Is the Fourth of July?," 23.

this trichotomy of signs, the icon is the *anthem*. The national anthem is that which signifies a sense, a quality that explains to America his identity. It is the narrative that America tells himself every day he wakes up in the morning. It is the inculcating principle by which he lives to rationalize his perceived predominance. It codifies a language for American exceptionalism. It is not constitutive of a constructive theology, or a redeemable philosophy, but rather a deconstructive solipsism. Here God is not present. What is present is a sense of unbounded worthiness and this strikingly in the presence of the racist intentionality of its lyrical composition. Note this emended verse from "The Star-Spangled Banner," written by Francis Scott Key, which reveals America's aversion to the very people it stole and forced into servitude, who sided with the British in battle to procure the freedom that was innately theirs:

> And where is that band who so vauntingly swore,
> That the havoc of war and the battle's confusion
> A home and a Country should leave us no more?
> Their blood has wash'd out their foul footstep's pollution.
> No refuge could save the hireling and slave
> From the terror of flight or the gloom of the grave,
> And the star-spangled banner in triumph doth wave
> O'er the land of the free and the home of the brave.[25]

This quality of morally vacant self-satisfaction extends from the anthem to the *index*, that which is rooted in a tangible reality, the *flag*. The flag for America is the vexillogical index that extends itself to the realism of American imperialism. Though, chronologically, the flag (partially sewn by an African American indentured servant girl)[26] was created before the anthem was written, it is the tangible and appreciable, concretized emblem of American world supremacy, a nation whose chief (Trump) denies the need for globalism, yet stipulates a global presence. The flag is waved high, saluted, pledged allegiance to. People drape their newborns in it, adorn their church sanctuaries with it, hang it in their classrooms, vociferously compelling their students to stand to honor it, and viciously denouncing anyone who does not celebrate it as a votive artifact. This is as close in proximity towards religiosity that America ever draws. This index is filled with

---

25. León, "National Anthem Is Racist."

26. "Indenture was a waning practice in early 19th Century Baltimore, although Maryland law did allow for courts to take away children of African Americas who were considered 'lazy, indolent, and worthless free negroes' to bind the youngsters into apprenticeship. Orphans usually met a similar fate" (Yuen and Boakyewa, "African American Girl").

and creates significations that are manifest and fraught—American chattel slavery, the practice of buying and selling human beings for profit, while dehumanizing the enslaved, forcing their labor with brutality, commoditizing their flesh, separating their families and destroying generations of lives— this institution of African enslavement existed for over 150 years before it was first conceived and sewn, and with it, years of domination, humiliation, deathly brutality finally had their tangible and textured manifestation, a flag. All the dehumanizing malintent, all the domineering rhetoric, all the brutality finally had its home in a gaudy artifact of cotton, hewn out of the blood of those it was meant to intimidate and destroy. Some of my fellow Southerners may argue that the Confederate flag, this artifact often philosophically aligned and flown alongside the Gadsden flag, the Thin Blue Line flag, the Trump: Keep America Great flags, and on occasion the Nazi flag, flown together in a chorus of tapestries, attached and afloat above the cargo bed of many a pick-up truck, is meant to symbolize states' rights against the encroachment of federal power. But the states' rights to own people as property is an evil imputed into the *index of the flag*, both the American and the Confederate, and it is a severe affront to the democracy that was victorious in the Civil War, whether they know it or not. And the American flag has yet to shake the evils signified in it through past generations of heaped injustices towards Black people because the nation that vaunts it refuses to deal with the continued injustices enacted against its Black citizens in the present.

The lionization of the flag as index, points toward the third of this series of significations, the symbol which is *patriotism*. This is a chauvinism that is at the center of America's wanton and virulent purblindness, which prohibits him from ever coming to terms with what he has been and presently is—a "moral monster."[27] This patriotism—this rigid patriotism—this patriotism that is concomitant with a vacuous, absent citizenship for Black people, this patriotism that is above reproach or redress, this patriotism that is above critique and suspicion, this patriotism that is the American god, this patriotism that contains all of the significations from the theology (index) of the flag, to the prayer (icon) of the anthem, is the god that is above all inquest, all thoughtful and systematic inquiry, and is the product of a

---

27. The term "moral monsters" is excerpted from an interview (showcased in the documentary *I Am Not Your Negro*) wherein the writer broods about the future of what he called the American Negro. He thinks about the "unthinking, cruel white majority," exclaiming that he is "terrified at the moral apathy, the death of the heart that is happening in [his] country." He ends this line of thought by suggesting that white people, the face and brain of America, "have diluted themselves for so long that they really don't think that I'm human . . . which means that they have become in themselves moral monsters" (Peck, *I Am Not Your Negro*).

person that wishes to dominate and oppress with immanent and doctrinal impunity.

Nevertheless, the hermeneutic enclosed in this essay must be explored by the preacher and layperson if they are ever to construct a theology of preaching, of cultivating a prophetic witness, that is truly liberative. For example, consider the text 2 Cor 10:4–5 KJV:

> (For the weapons of our warfare are not carnal, but mighty through God to the pulling down of strong holds;) casting down imaginations, and every high thing that exalteth itself against the knowledge of God, and bringing into captivity every thought to the obedience of Christ.

There are preachers out there who would use this text as the site to construct a homily steeped in evangelical piety filled with pabulum platitudes about the "thought-life of the believer" and how we as Christians need to pull down the strongholds of sin, particularly sexual immorality, from our lives if we are ever going to live into our "purpose." I can hear this sermon in my head even now. However, the preacher informed by the textual resistance of the Black lived experience, a hermeneutic posture bent always towards justice and equity, would rather use this text as an opportunity to liberate. For example, rather than echoing a series of pious talking points around an issue of an invisible sin, it would be so much more advantageous to speak to the matter of pulling down Confederate monuments that are, in fact, representative of an imagination that exalts itself against the knowledge of God. If one, preacher or not, were about the work of liberation and adopted this hermeneutic posture in life, then one would look at this text as a moment of pulling down (not a supposed stronghold of consensual acts between men and women or men and men or women and women, transgender or otherwise, in the privacy of their own home) a police force that enables its officers to murder unarmed Black people in the streets, and then one would seek amelioration through the abolition (pulling down/casting down) of such a police force through gradual defunding and divesting. Then there could be a view towards a more just and verdant future for the society where there is not overpolicing, a product of overfunding of police, but of community enrichment made possible by the divested funds from the bloated budgets of police departments in cities across the nation.

Therefore, if the preacher is indeed concerned with preaching liberation and beatification, the preacher would adopt this hermeneutic posture, one informed by the especial ontological triumphal experience of Black people in America and one that is able to interrogate the ways in which a great nihilism has swept through the oppressed populations of the nation, particularly that of Black peoples, from generation to generation of state-sanctioned disenfranchisement and mistreatment, that does not indict the protestor or looter in favor of those who uphold the systems that they are protesting. Cornel West speaks to this sense of nihilism in his *Race Matters*:

> The liberal/conservative discussion conceals the most basic issue now facing Black America: *the nihilistic threat to its very existence*. This threat is not simply a matter of relative economic deprivation and political powerlessness—though economic well-being and political clout are requisites for meaningful Black progress. It is primarily speaking to the profound sense of psychological depression, personal worthlessness, and social despair so widespread in Black America.[28]

For example, in Portsmouth, Virginia, where I am from, crime is a problem, particularly violent crime. Violent crime is such a problem, in fact, that in Portsmouth the chance of becoming a victim of either violent or property crime is one in fifteen,[29] this in a city of just over 95,000 residents. I grew up in Portsmouth. As a grown man looking back, knowing the statistical data that I know now about how dangerous my city was (and continues to be), I marvel that I made it out unscathed. I have never been the victim of violent crime, though I have known people who were shot and killed, one while eating with his family inside a Wendy's. I think about how, in 2016, Virginia Beach incurred 700 cases of violent crimes and Portsmouth incurred 758 cases of violent crimes; however, the major difference between the two cities in this regard is that, while their number of violent crimes were similar, Virginia Beach happens to be the most populous city in all of Virginia, having that year some 453,017 residents. The number of residents living in Portsmouth that same year? 95, 813.[30]

Nevertheless, somehow, the closest I ever did come to being a victim of violent crime in Portsmouth was one day at afterschool marching band rehearsal when, in broad daylight, some assailants began shooting across the street from my high school (located in the heart of downtown Portsmouth). We saw them run away dressed in all black, as our band director shouted to us, "Run to the band room!" I think about this and I am reminded of how improbable my trajectory has been, matriculating as a student at Boston University School of Theology. Not only because I survived growing up in Portsmouth City, senses untrammeled, body unscarred, mentality sane, but also that the plight of Black people in general, and Black men, in America, is

---

28. West, *Race Matters*, 12–13.
29. "Portsmouth, VA: Crime Rates," para. 1.
30. "Portsmouth, VA: Crime Rates," para. 1.

and has always been precarious. It is not lost on me that I was the only Black man in the 2018–2019 Master of Sacred Theology cohort. Further, it is not lost on me that I was the only Black man living in the School of Theology's subsidized housing (Beane House) for that school year. Further still, it is not lost on me that I was one of only eight Black male students in the entire School of Theology (I do not include African immigrants in this number; I speak only of those descendants of the African enslaved in America). It very much could have been me in that statistical number of decedents; yet here I am. I have not been made involuntarily absent like so many of those who look like me in this country, and for that I am grateful and motivated.

In America, Black men have been admitted to state prison on drug charges at a rate that is more than thirteen times higher than white men.[31] The racial bias inherent in the drug war is a major reason that one in every fourteen Black men was behind bars in 2006, compared with one in 106 white men.[32] For younger Black men, the statistics are even worse. One in nine Black men between the ages of twenty and thirty-five was behind bars in 2006, and far more were under some form of penal control—such as probation or parole.[33] Black people are four times more likely to die of the novel coronavirus that is literally plaguing the nation.[34] Still, if this veritable misery march were not dire enough, Black people in America are still twice more likely to be killed by the police, and this number has not changed during the COVID-19 pandemic quarantine,[35] a fact revealed by the murders of George Floyd, Breonna Taylor, Ahmaud Arbery, Tony McDade, Rayshard Brooks, and too many others.

All these figures are demonstrative of an attempt to create a new racial undercaste amongst Black persons living in America. There is a groan that Black people carry in their throats that murmurs in stillness under the immenseness of social, economic, and political inequities and corporate hypocrisy and greed. This painfully quiescent murmur can become the shout of a prophetic witness, giving way to a prophetic voice, if the textuality of this lived experience can be allowed to inform the sensibilities of preachers, even those who are not Black, even those who are not typical preachers.

So why would I, a Black man, want or need to hear a sermon that parrots the same normative thinking that reinforces a spirituality consequential of invisible threats flying about in the air up there somewhere, when there

31. Alexander, *New Jim Crow*, 100.
32. Alexander, *New Jim Crow*, 100.
33. Alexander, *New Jim Crow*, 100.
34. Booth and Barr, "Black People Four Times More Likely."
35. "Police Shootings Database," para. 1.

are very real and fungible strongholds down here in the form of monuments, in the form of flags flying visibly from major interstate arteries, in the form of street names, in the form of racist housing policies, in the form of police brutality predicated and reinforced by written systems of procedural impunity? The answer is that I would not. I need a word that does not even have to emerge from a pulpit, but that can come from any realm of society—a word that seeks justice, that loves mercy, that employs a hermeneutic that wholly resists any method of interpretation of texts that continues to perpetrate violence in one way or another against Black people.

WHAT I MEAN BY TEXTUALITY—CHALLENGES OF LIVING IN A TEXTUAL WORLD

Paul Ricœur theorized that there is natural distanciation and estrangement in any text and that to make this distanciation and estrangement that naturally occurs in the text productive for oneself is interpretation. He writes:

> Interpretation, philosophically understood, is nothing else than an attempt to make estrangement and distanciation productive.[36]

And again, he writes:

> This dialectic has an existential overtone. Distanciation meant above all estrangement, and appropriation was intended as the "remedy" which could "rescue" cultural heritages of the past from the alienation of distance.[37]

This methodology is for Ricœur a modus operandi for reunifying the interlocutor with the text to impart a new self into the ego of the interpreter of the text through appropriation. However, perhaps Ricœur's theoretical outlook has an ambition that is not productive after all, because it would be a model of interpretation mediated and informed by the interlocutor's own epistemological and ontological biases, biases that would oft prevent her from interpreting texts in a way mindful of an experience that would be a debasement or dislocation of her own. Likewise, for the Black person in America, it would not be at all profitable or expedient to adopt Ricœur's analysis of the purpose or aim of this brand of interpretation for obvious reasons. To make the estrangement and distanciation in the text meaningful for the Black person would no doubt mean assimilation to the tenets of the text and therefore would mean that the Black person again would be

---

36. Ricœur, *Interpretation Theory*, 4.
37. Ricœur, *Interpretation Theory*, 89.

subjugated by the text's originary intent. Furthermore, to allow the text to impart a new self into the ego as mode of transformative textual appropriation is dangerous. Why would the Black person ever wish to allow the texts from the past, especially in the Western canon, to impart a new self into her ego? This would no doubt be delimiting, degrading, and deleting. However, what if this new self is an ontological presence that is ever in posture to reject and resist the textual frameworks of historicism? To this end, Ricœur posits:

> This link between disclosure and appropriation is, to my mind, the cornerstone of a hermeneutic which would claim both to overcome the shortcomings of historicism and to remain faithful to the original intention of Schleiermacher's hermeneutics.[38]

This is the essence of the hermeneutic at the core of my theology of preaching: a theology that is informed by a Ricœurian ethos, one that makes real the existential overtones of textuality and that has adopted as an observable mode of ontological presence to prepare the interlocutor with the text to always point towards restoration and liberation, not degradation and humiliation, rejecting the painful historicism of past intentionality with motility towards a freer future. It is a hermeneutically disclosed theology of preaching that observes all "the semantic autonomy of written discourse and the self-contained existence of the literary work . . . ultimately grounded in the objectivity of meaning of oral discourse itself,"[39] resistant to narrativity that absolves culpability of insidious political actors and established hierarchichalism, which results in an economic underclass. It is a highly contextual spiritual work, one that seeks to ameliorate the problematizations of a theological hermeneutic that foregrounds self-aggrandizement and deplores self-actualization.

This first step is for the purpose of reunifying the reader (especially in my homiletical intentionality) and the preacher with the text, by causing the preacher to see herself textually. The second step is to prove that in the thinking of Ricœur there is natural distanciation and estrangement from any text that must be appropriated in a meaningful way to be interpreted aright. Therefore, if the preacher can understand herself as a text, not discounting her especial experience (even if it is one of marginality), it will make the processes of making the inherent estrangement in a text productive, and her interpretation of the text stronger. *Textuality* is what this phenomenon is called, and this is the *self* of Ricœur that will be imparted into the ego upon

---

38. Ricœur, *Interpretation Theory*, 93.
39. Ricœur, *Interpretation Theory*, 91.

making the text meaningful to oneself. This is an attempt to reengage and reunify the preacher with the inherently alienated text so that the preacher reading better, with the aim and motivation of liberation preaching, will preach better and that justice will be the perlocutionary apotheosis.

THE ILLOCUTIONARY PROBLEMATICS OF AN ANTI-LIBERATION HERMENEUTIC

What is the intent of this speech act device that is the hermeneutic posture of an ontological resistance to insidious textuality? It is that an experience, namely that experience of the Black person, might be used as a heuristic to inform the sensibilities of all preachers. This is what Ricœur referred to as the miracle of dialogue as communication:

> My experience cannot directly become your experience. An event belonging to one stream of consciousness cannot be transferred as such into another stream of consciousness. Yet, nevertheless, something passes from me to you. Something is transferred from one sphere of life to another. This something is not the experience as experienced, but its meaning. Here is the miracle. The experience as experienced, as lived, remains private, but its sense, its meaning, becomes public. Communication in this way is the overcoming of the radical non-communicability of the lived experience as lived.[40]

The term homiletics, the art of preaching, comes from the Greek word *homilein*, which means converse with. Conversing with someone is dialogue. Preaching is but a dialogue, the most august dialogue there is. From the preached word, like any dialogue, the experience is easily transferred. Therefore, this modality of thinking about one's relation to text regarding resistance to text is so important. If there is no speech act, this hermeneutic can never be made manifest. This miracle that affords my own private experience to be made public is real. However, if my own private experience is not one that is in resistance and open rebellion against those oppressive powers that seek to denigrate, deracinate, and denude the body politic, what I communicate will no doubt be hampered by the myopathy of that ineffectual lived perspective. In this way, the lived experience of Black ontological fightback gives new definition and grants fervid vitality to Ricœur's explanation of dialogue.

---

40. Ricœur, *Interpretation Theory*, 16.

Woe is me if I preach not the Gospel! The concealment of the locutionary promise informed by four hundred years of responsible resistance to oppression comes through absolutely in my existential experience. This theology of preaching is highly mediated by an experience that can never be actualized if not spoken in the speech act of the preached word, be it in proclamation from the pulpit or a prophetic witness in the public sphere. There is a promise that becomes greater in substance when the preachment emerges from this hermeneutic of resistance to abhorrent textuality: there is a promise ensconced here in the locutionary act of speech where the parole of the locution has in it an intent (the illocutionary act of the speech), and the effect of the intent is demonstrated in the perlocutionary act of the speech. Without these as part and parcel of the preached word, this invaluable lived experience, as such theology of preaching, can never be fully known. This is highly contextual preaching, and the meaning must be made manifest. The existential meaning of the Black person must be made known to the benefit and boon of the preacher or laity, and as a sacred repository of all theologies of preaching—an ontologically informed hermeneutical posture that lends itself intrinsically and immediately to the practice of liberation made manifest through preaching or civic engagement, changing lives, and altering futures. A theology of voice (*Saved from Silence: Finding Women's Voice in Preaching*) becomes meaningless if the voice is not vectored towards the total liberation of all marginalized peoples. A theology of the whispered word (*Whispered Word: A Theology of Preaching*) becomes insignificant when whispering for some is optional and for others is a mandatory reality of subjugation. A theology of Black liberation is stifled and stymied, if only Black, cisgender, heteronormative men are made central to it, denying the anthropological concerns of Black women, Black LGBTQIA, and Black transgender people.

In short, if this hermeneutical approach towards liberation of oppressed peoples is never made manifest, justice for *all* can never be achieved. If your hermeneutic posture is already set towards the work of liberation and beatification, then it will be more readily available to call upon for an interpretation of the Sacred Text that rejects texts that preclude or occlude the vital, especial values of all peoples. If this hermeneutic posture is embraced, it will position its adherents towards an approach to resisting hegemonic codes of society at large that hierarchicalizes and prioritizes white people over Black people, rich over poor, man over woman, and cisgender/heteronormative over transgender/homosexual. It is my desire that with this hermeneutic move there can be learned from a fundament of liberation hermeneutics of preaching that can be extended and transferred from the Black lived experience in America to the white lived experience in America, how this Black textual resistance can be made manifest and transferred to a white phenomenology to help generate what Ibram X. Kendi calls antiracism (however, once a person decides to inhabit his or her whiteness, it becomes very difficult not to be racist, for the creation of whiteness as ecology, as property, was for the express purpose of racism and domination).[41] Put simply, text as the means of justice and a hermeneutic posture informed by the specific experience of Black people in America is the pathway through which this justice can emerge. You do not have to be a preacher to appreciate or glean from this essay: the topic of preaching for me is simply the most generative and constructive because of how, weekly, in constancy, the preacher more than most must deal directly and intently with text and apply a hermeneutic to a text that, when developed prior to and rendered to an awaiting congregation, will have either potentially debilitating or ameliorating effects, making the preacher an invaluable interlocutor about the matter of textuality.

Therefore, in closing, let us look at another biblical text to illumine the beauty of Blackness as the site of textual resistance and redemptive hermeneutic posture.

The following is a very familiar text from one of the epistles accredited to the apostle John. This is one of my favorite Bible verses because it speaks to how important cultivating fellowship is to God, and it redounds to how significant it is to God to maintain right relations, without strife, without acrimony, how there can be forgiveness and healing even when we may not believe we are worthy of ablution. However, I have often seen/heard this verse be used to communicate the intractability of certain acts being unpardonable, particularly suicide:

> If we confess our sins, he is faithful and just to forgive us our sins, and to cleanse us from all unrighteousness.[42]

Many preachers will use this text to promote the ideation that the killing of oneself will automatically condemn one to a devil's hell, using the untried and unthought rationale that, according to the face-value of the text, if it is so that the only way one's sins can be forgiven is to confess the sin openly, then such an act would be impossible after killing oneself. Therefore, no

---

41. This is why white people can slip in and out of racism and why antiracism has its limitations, because what needs to be confronted is not simply racism as ideology but racism as white supremacist ecology, which has its own inalienable laws and features. As long as this ecology exists, no one will be able to be antiracist because the allure of domination is too centralized in ideas of whiteness. It is a world ecology that affords too much power to be willfully relinquished.

42. 1 John 1:19 KJV.

forgiveness; therefore, condemnation. The falsely dichotomous reasoning of this fallacy aside, three questions emerge from considering how delimiting a similar hermeneutic applied to this text would be: 1) Why must it be so that suicide must indeed be a sin? 2) Is this notion of suicide's "sin-ness" applicable to all situations? 3) If not, then how can it be considered a useful and just interpretation of this text at all? Rather, this hermeneutical posture proffers only a winnowed, myopic view of text, simply parroting old theological traditions, many of which uphold and sustain hierarchies and hegemonies of culture and serve to keep a growing underclass ultimately subservient instead of offering a newer way of reading text that fosters justice, that allows the particular and especial claims and scenarios of lives outside the so-called dominant culture to be mindfully considered, appraised, and substantiated.

For example, historically, for Black people in this country, or en route to this country against their will in the holds of slaver ships, suicide has never been opprobrious or anathema, certainly never *sin*. It has existed for us as a way to reclaim our righteousness, to reclaim our peace, to reclaim our selfhood. This is a point that Joshua Bennett makes in his fantastic monograph *Being Property Once Myself: Blackness and the End of Man*. In it he theorizes how the literary imagination of Black authors exemplified through the deft and pointed use of animality in their works avails itself to locating new ways of exploring interspecies/intraspecies relationalism and exploding hierarchichalism in society at large, through perspectives on African American ontology, maleness/masculinity, femininity, free moral agency, ecopoetics, and love. Each chapter of the book focuses on a different animal and how an author discloses the uncanny significations of the animal in a particular work of fiction or nonfiction or poetry: Introduction—"Horse," *Narrative of the Life of Frederick Douglass* by Frederick Douglass; Chapter 1—"Rat," *Native Son* by Richard Wright; Chapter 2—"Cock," *Song of Solomon* by Toni Morrison; Chapter 3—"Mule," *Their Eyes Were Watching God* by Zora Neale Hurston; Chapter 4—"Dog," *Salvage the Bones* by Jesmyn Ward; Chapter 5—"Shark," "Middle Passage" by Robert Hayden and "The Sea-Turtle and the Shark" by Melvin B. Tolson. Of best use here is Chapter 5, which focuses on Melvin B. Tolson's and Robert Hayden's use of the *shark* to speak metonymically about the slaver's brutality towards the African in bonded transit to the New World and metaphorically about the representation of the Atlantic Ocean as a means of unmoored territory within which to transfigure a newer, freer being. Most relevant here for discussion is Bennett's analysis of Hayden's poem "Middle Passage," the setting of which is the infamous Spanish slaver ship, *La Amistad*:

I
Jesús, Estrella, Esperanza, Mercy:
  Sails flashing to the wind like weapons,
  sharks following the moans the fever and the dying;
  horror the corposant and compass rose.
Middle Passage:
        voyage through death
                to life upon these shores.
"10 April 1800—
Blacks rebellious. Crew uneasy. Our linguist says
their moaning is a prayer for death,
ours and their own. Some try to starve themselves.
Lost three this morning leaped with crazy laughter
to the waiting sharks, sang as they went under."[43]

Bennett, whose own work deals with a kind of resistance to implicit Western patriarchal normatives of being, observes that the "sharks in this [opening scene of the poem] are merely one component of a larger network of ultra-violent actors," that they are part and parcel of a system that is actively working against Black life. Deep into his analysis, Bennett suggests that the very presence of the sharks in the poem empowers the captive to "*[steal] oneself away*, refusing to become the property of another even if that choice ends in death," how the sharks function "as a kind of specter, both an ever-looming threat to the flourishing of black life and a release valve, a guaranteed exit," how "in West African cosmologies and spiritual practice . . . their vision of what it might mean to steal away . . . saw biological death not as an absolute conclusion but rather as a means of returning to one's native land," how stealing oneself away "was a refusal of objectification, an unmooring of the relentless, necromantic machinations of a global order that demanded human beings be transformed into saleable commodities."[44] Notice what tends here is the sanctity of life secured in the self-initiation of one's own death: to accept the narrativized reality that one is property, that one is a slave, would mean death—psychical death, spiritual death, physical death—a very literal suicide. Therefore, using Bennett's literary analysis of Hayden's poem, we can reconfigure our orientation towards the act of suicide, not from a place of privilege, but from a hermeneutic posture that lends itself to the specific historical experience of Black people, a hermeneutic posture that decenters hegemony of interpretation and uplifts the especial experience of those considered to be on the margins of society as equally viable. Now, after mindfully enacting this hermeneutical move, we can begin interpreting

43. Hayden, "Middle Passage," in *Collected Poems*, lines 1–13.
44. Bennett, *Being Property Once Myself*, 177.

the text in a relevant way by asking relevant questions like "What could be holier than an African killing himself by throwing himself off the decks of a slaver's ship with a shout of joy and with laughter?" For how could that ever be considered a sin? What could be holier than a man reclaiming his free moral agency, reclaiming his subjectivity, reclaiming his autonomy, while simultaneously depriving his enslaver of a part of his projected workforce, whereby crippling his heinous, vile economic earnings? Few things come to mind at the ready more heavenly than that.

I want to be clear that I do not advocate suicide, physical or philosophical; I want to offer a redemptive modalism of interpretation, of both actions and actors, of thought, particularly that of Black people, to lift that specific experience to the fore as the site for justice, as the site from whence a newer, freer world can become possible.[45] This analysis of a poem, unfurling roundabout the very real events of a real slaver's ship, illustrates how Black people have always been resistant in their ontology, in their very being, to the ways in which society has textually circumscribed them in this country. The slaves on the ship were written off as property. But by killing themselves they made a claim of humanity that could not be taken from them. This is like how Tillich describes Socrates and his executioners in *The Courage to Be*:

> In Stoicism and Neo-Stoicism the essential self is not threatened by death, because it belongs to being-itself and transcends non-being. Socrates, who in the power of his essential self conquered the anxiety of death, has become the symbol for the courage to take death upon oneself. This is the true meaning of Plato's so-called doctrine of immortality of the soul. In discussing this doctrine we should neglect the arguments for the dying Socrates. All the arguments, skeptically treated by Plato himself, are attempts to interpret the courage of Socrates, the courage to take one's own death into one's self-affirmation. Socrates is

---

45. There is so much more to Blackness than struggle against whiteness (whiteness as a metaphor for power, whiteness as metonymy for domination) and white supremacy. If there is not, then that would mean that whiteness is what gives Blackness its essence, that it undergirds its very formation—and that could never be so. This is the central thesis of Victor Anderson's great book *Beyond Ontological Blackness*, and I think it is a necessary point to make here. What I have attempted with this essay is to demonstrate how Blackness in all of its multivariateness is capacious enough to be exemplar of resistance to hegemony and domination as immanent existential mode of praxis that could be profitable to all and how Blackness, in its infallibility and indestructibility, is free to act in its own interests: if the Black person desires to throw her hat in the ring to confront white supremacy in all its forms headlong, fine; if the Black person decides not to, for whatever reason, fine. It does not obviate these necessary lessons that can be learned from the Black experience in America.

certain that the self which the executioners will destroy is not the self which affirms itself in his courage to be. He does not say much about the relation of the two selves, and he could not because they are not numerically two, but one in two aspects. But he makes it clear that the courage to die is the test of the courage to be.[46]

By taking one's own life into one's own hands with aplomb like the captured Africans did on the *Amistad*, one claims for oneself, through the self-affirmation of autonomy, a *self* that can never be taken away, one that the executioner cannot find, one that sharks cannot find, one that the Atlantic Ocean cannot find, one that racist police officers cannot find, one that the white supremacist textual world of America cannot find. This is the legacy of Blackness as mode of resistance. It is effective, it is immortal, it is indestructible—*Blackness*. So, we see that Blackness is not only the site of justice (justice as the creation of access—access to healthy, whole foods, access to affordable housing and healthcare, access to profitable education, access to arts programs, etc., for underserved groups across the country) but in its pursuit of justice through textual resistance, it also reveals its power as imperishable. The indestructible character of this hermeneutic speaks to its durability not to be consumed in the four-hundred-year-old cauldron of white supremacist racism and bigotry but to ascend it always, to thrive despite it, to live beyond it.

46. Tillich, *Courage to Be*, 204.

4.

Slavoj Žižek and Being Racially Profiled

Black men are the summary of weight.
—AFAA MICHAEL WEAVER, "AMERICAN INCOME"

It was twice in one night. Has to be a record or something. A personal best, in the very least. One of my friends said that I should not have bought the book, that I should have left it there in repose on the green counter at that Barnes and Noble. But I have never been one to satisfyingly explode on a deserving recipient of my rage. The unbridled furor seethes for a time thereafter, me wishing with all my might that I had told the unfortunate person about himself.

Being profiled is always a strange occurrence. It always takes me back to that time when I was nineteen, and the police decided that I was too young and too Black to be driving a Mercedes-Benz.

Being pulled over by the police is never a pleasant experience. I never know what to do with my hands. And, of course, I don't want to be shot (no one ever really does!). I prefer 10 and 2. I think to myself it feels like a 10 and 2 kind of a night.

"Is there a problem, officer?" rattles off my tongue with the ease of my first breath into the world.

Long as I live I will never ask a more meaningless question.

But this is Chesapeake.

I hear through the corridors of space-time my father's bellowing, prevenient instruction, his voice adding to the panoply of feelings swishing around the chamber pot of my disgust—a static and miserable ambedo—

"If you ever get pulled over by the cops. Don't make any sudden movements. Be respectful. Keep your hands where he can see them."

A song I know by heart but never had to perform until now.

"Step out of the car."

The officer plunges an ultimatum into my eye.

Now, if I were speeding (I was), why not simply write me a ticket for my transgression, keeper of the law? Why suggest that if I allow you to search my Mercedes you'll just let me go?

No, I'm not from this area. No, I don't sell crack.

I am only three minutes from home. I am on my dad's insurance. I don't want his rate to go up. Go ahead. Ruin my leather seats. I just conditioned them. Too young. Don't know my rights yet. But he knew them.

He lets me go.

How is it that some people must follow the law and others do not? If it were in service of the law to issue me a speeding ticket, why not simply do so? But there is constantly at work a religious allegiance to a system of codified exaltation on one hand and diminishment on the other, written into the very fabric of American society, so pervasive that even legal apparatuses cannot justly function.

What is most bizarre about it, being racially profiled, is that in a sense it is mostly classist and greatly economical; yet, the person doing the profiling often makes less money than I do in a year, working for a barely livable wage in a highly marketized low-morale, corporate apparatus that cares nothing about him or her as a person. To complexify matters even more is that both of the women who profiled me that evening had no dog in the fight, stood to make no more money than they did for hastily generalizing me based on the merits of my skin color—there was no bonus coming their way, yet they felt somehow empowered by either the Kroger paraphernalia to accost me with probing, lidless stares at self-checkout or ask me for my receipt at a bookstore for a book I brought with me from home to read there while buying another book (which also shows the bare unthinking stupidity of racial profiling—Would you steal a book while purchasing another book? Wouldn't the good thief just walk out with both books? Why waste time paying for a book with legal tender? You're not even being honest with yourself at this point. But, as I have discussed in another essay, racism as such, as the ecology of white supremacy as religion, has no thought applied. It is a mindless, thoughtless, affective way of life that requires no interrogation of one's motives.). Can their allegiance be bought so cheaply at the price of $7.25–8.50/hr. to dehumanize a patron, or are they just so piteously entrenched and dedicated to their purblind bigotry that they are unable to see the futility in their ideological pursuit, a point Žižek discloses in his book

The Sublime Object of Ideology, speaking to the conceptual subconscious implications of anti-Semitism as a meaningless ideology:

> Let us suppose, for example, that an objective look would confirm—why not?—that Jews really do financially exploit the rest of the population, that they do sometimes seduce our young daughters, that some of them do not wash regularly. Is it not clear that this has nothing to do with the real roots of anti-Semitism? Here, we have only to remember the Lacanian proposition concerning the pathologically jealous husband: even if all the facts he quotes in support of his jealousy are true, even if his wife really is sleeping around with other men, this does not change one bit the fact that his jealousy is a pathological, paranoid construction.

He adds:

> Let us ask ourselves a simple question: in the Germany of the late 1930s, what would be the result of such a non-ideological, objective approach? Probably something like: "The Nazis are condemning Jews too hastily, without proper argument, so let us take a cool, sober look and see if they are really guilty or not; let us see if there is some truth in the accusations against them." Is it really necessary to add that such an approach would merely confirm our so-called "unconscious prejudices" with additional rationalizations? The proper answer to anti-Semitism is therefore not "Jews are really not like that" but "the anti-Semitic idea of Jew has nothing to do with Jews; the ideological figure of a Jew is a way to stitch up the inconsistency of our own ideological system."[1]

Maintaining a watchful eye on Black customers for no other reason than that they are Black, looking for some confirmation that Black people are, in fact, thieving, conniving miscreants, can never be justified on the ideological level because it is innately in pursuit of something that never even existed in the first place. Ideology is in search of an object, then deigns to think that it can attain it. It is the Lacanian *objet petit a*, the veritable unattainable object that is the pursuit of all ideology, as recounted by Žižek in his discourse of William Tenn's *The Discovery of Morniel Mathaway*:

> A distinguished art historian takes a journey in a time machine from the twenty-fifth century to our day to visit and study *in vivo* the immortal Morniel Mathaway, a painter not appreciated

---

1. Žižek, *Sublime Object of Ideology*, 49.

in our time but later discovered to have been the greatest painter of the era. When he encounters him, the art historian finds no trace of a genius, just an imposter, a megalomaniac, even a swindler who steals his time machine from him and escapes to the future, so that poor art historian stays tied to our time. The only action open to him is to assume the identity of the escaped Mathaway and to paint under his name all his masterpieces that he remembers from the future—it is he himself who is really the misrecognized genius he was looking for![2]

The art historian was that which he had sought after and idolized the entire time. Žižek continues:

> This, therefore, is the basic paradox we are aiming at: the subject is confronted with a scene from the past that he wants to change, to meddle with, to intervene in; he takes a journey into the past, intervenes in the scene, and it is not that he "cannot change anything"—quite the contrary, only through his intervention does the scene from the past *become what it always was*: his intervention was from the beginning compromised, included. The initial "illusion" of the subject consists in simply forgetting to include in the scene his own act—that is, to overlook how "it counts, it is counted, and the one who counts is already included in the account."[3]

What this parable reveals is not only that the art historian was sufficient in himself and that he needed not to look to anyone as an archetype toward which to turn his envious fervor, but also that what we think our ideology serves us to obtain is nonexistent. Again, ideology is in search of an object, deigning to think that it can attain it, that it is sublime and resplendent:

> An ordinary, everyday act becomes impossible to accomplish as soon as it finds itself occupying the impossible place of *das Ding* and begins to embody the sublime object of desire. This object or act may be in itself extremely banal (a common dinner, passing the threshold after a party). It has only to occupy the sacred/forbidden, empty place in the Other, and a whole series of impassable obstacles will build up around it; the object or act, in its very vulgarity cannot be reached or accomplished.[4]

---

2. Žižek, *Sublime Object of Ideology*, 60.
3. Žižek, *Sublime Object of Ideology*, 60.
4. Žižek, *Sublime Object of Ideology*, 221.

It is never sufficient to respond to the ideology of white supremacy in any of its permutations with an ideology, but rather with good theology. This is because theology does not look to attain some sublime object but is always in pursuit, not counting itself the capacity to ever arrive at what it pursues yet being fulfilled in the process. The apostle Paul expressed it this way in his letter to the church at Philippi:

> Not as though I had already attained, either were already perfect: but I follow after, if that I may apprehend that for which also I am apprehended of Christ. Brethren, I count not myself to have apprehended: but this one thing I do, forgetting those things which are behind, and reaching forth unto those things which are before, I press toward the mark for the prize of the high calling of God in Christ Jesus.[5]

Though, one thing remains: the year is 2020. I am in a self-checkout lane. I am thinking about the sweetness of the frozen dragonfruit I just scanned over the sensor and how well it will blend with the kale I have at home. I watch the pretty girl behind the customer service desk assisting a patron in the distance. I will later learn that she's eighteen. A pity. She'll think I'm twenty-two. The compliment will fail to anesthetize me from the pain that preceded it. I feel the glower of a stare against my bearded cheek, in substance groping my testicles from a free throw line's distance away. Suddenly, I am eighteen again, stopped and frisked in the swelter of a summer's night with a frightened girlfriend I could not protect. It unnerves me. I make eye contact with the assailant. Her eyes are too close together. Later, I will be in the foyer of my home petting my dog I raised from a pup who blithely greeted me at the door upon entry, wondering to myself who deputized a cashier with the authority to ruin someone's night, if she knew that I was worthy of the affection of canine licks and wagging tail, that I had a warm touch informed by a heart that never beat towards theft. Days from now, writing lesson plans, an image from this incident will harass my memory. This is what it looks like to be a pillar of my community.

---

5. Phil 3:13 NRSV.

Interlude

BLACK HISTORY

Last night

I had a dream then
awoke in
Matthew Henson's
back yard
he said
through bristled jaw
that I saved an Inuit child
from exposure   to cold

the child did not thank me

I am too dark
to see
gratitude

was born
by a river

was sold
to merchants

followed the
drinking gourd

nursed my
ankles with blood

sopped hard
tack with tears

bought my
wife a body

choked on Jim's
Crow for dinner

marched on
good intentions

slept with
corner office
thought
I had a dream

thought it
was a dream

awoke into pale light

clear skies do not always signal peace

somewhere right now
I lie face down
taking my last
breath to the head

with eyes like
empty promises

& the sky
could not be
bluer

5.

White Supremacy Is a Religion

Oh no, he ain' dead. De signs an' de tokens tells me.

—LIZA JANE IN CHESNUTT, THE WIFE OF HIS YOUTH

Black people in America have always believed in signs. Certainly, the Black person was once stipulated to have this belief, using signs to abscond the brutalism of her forced bondage, following drinking gourds, emblazoning stars in her eyes, the silver moon no mere cosmological phantom to her but a veritable pillar of cloud by day and a fire by night. Indeed, be they in the heavens above or in our dreams at night, we all look for signs for comfort, for the assurance that things will improve, to corroborate that we are who we reckon we are, to affirm that which we already know to be true. In his short story "The Wife of His Youth," largely unsung African American author Charles Waddell Chesnutt narratively illustrates a portrait of an indomitable woman in search of her long-lost husband, from whom she was separated when he ran away to the North, from enslavement, with the promise he would return for her a free man to ransom her, never to do so. Following Emancipation, searching up and down the East Coast on foot looking for her husband, a woman, a senescent woman, a senescent Black woman with no help, no reason to hope, confesses to Mr. Ryder that she knew her Sam was still alive because she saw it in the *signs*.[1]

In "Of Our Spiritual Strivings," the seminal first chapter of W. E. B. Du Bois's magnum opus *The Souls of Black Folk*, the author muses upon the

---

1. Chesnutt, "Wife of His Youth," 550.

ways that it feels for him as a Black man "to be a problem."[2] Here he examines the ways in which the Black presence is an inconvenience. For Du Bois, the most striking and shocking revelation of his life was that, though white people surrounded him, and he was embroiled roundabout by whiteness, excelling in the face of his pallid classmates, he himself was not white, and that this dearth of whiteness was in fact a deficit to him. This ever appeared to him anathema, opprobrious, an obstruction to the innate justice that would be his non-presence, something that wrenched him; for to not exist is a problematic that he, existing, just could not overcome. For to be present is to affront, to be present is enough to mitigate, to warrant the aversive response to the stimuli of his unabashedly unchained ontology. He, a priori the startling revelation of his Blackness as mode of undesirable difference, had borne no distinction necessitated to overcome until he was confronted by a peer—a "girl, a tall newcomer, [who] refused [his] card—refused it peremptorily, with a glance."[3] It was at this precise moment that he knew that his very heartbeat, his organs, his senses, his affections, his passions, those very things that contributed to his humanity could neither assuage nor mollify the unremitting chasm of race. Therefore, in Du Bois's mind, the need for the double consciousness of the Black person in America is immediate and tethered dutifully to her ontic composition. It is in this way solely for defense, a defense without which the Black person could not survive, much less exist.

Consequently, according to Cécile Laborde in her book *Liberalism's Religion,* there should be a range of permissible secularisms, that she terms minimal secularism, and the ideal that should undergird a liberal-democratic society like America should be constitutive of an inclusive state secularism where the government does not abet or promote any certain religion as being more prominent than another, that it "should not endorse *any* orthodoxy that might have disparaging effects on some citizens."[4] Doing so would engender less ability for separation of secularism in the state, and Laborde's thesis in *Liberalism's Religion* is that religion and the state can coexist, or rather, do not require too strict a separation, if there are certain minimal secularisms applied to its governmental morphology. However, this is problematic in America because white supremacy *is* its religion, in fact it is *the* religion, and it is the religion that is and has been upheld in America since the dawning of the republic, having its first liturgy in the genocide of indigenous peoples and later in chattel slavery.

2. Du Bois, *Souls of Black Folk*, 2.
3. Du Bois, *Souls of Black Folk*, 3.
4. Laborde, *Liberalism's Religion*, 94.

Why *religion*? Why that seemingly stilted terminology to describe an ideology of superiority? Surely there must be other ways of describing the phenomenon of white supremacy, ways that do not seem to insist on the sensational. Yet, this is no sensationalist appeal or alarmist demagoguery, this description is rooted in the tangible facticity of white supremacy in America. White supremacy in America is a highly systematized, ritualized program of being, filled with dedication and devotion (like that found in the adherents of world religions like Islam, Buddhism, Judaism, Shintoism, Taoism, Sikhism, Catholicism, Hinduism, Protestant Christianity, et al.) that is reminiscent of a faith-based tradition and instituted by greed, routinized by policy, emboldened by quietly radicalized adherents.

Is it so dubious? Is it so unimaginable? Is it so fantastical? Is it so hard to seem that there is in place in this country a religion that adheres to the consciousness that Black people are subhuman, that still holds that Black people are three-fifths human, are nothing more than slaves? This is why an uprising is characterized as a riot. This is why Chicagoans are scapegoated as indicative of Black people's supposed penchant for destructiveness and are characterized as savages. It is not jihadist Islam, it is not radical Central African Catholicism. It, white supremacy as religion, is not aberrant as many suppose, the activity of some lone actors, who are abstracted from the realities of a trenchant past that motivates the actions of the present. Rather, it is an ecology of the prescription of whiteness as economic and sociological power and infrastructural discrimination that has strengthened and encouraged many to live into its promises of exceptionalism, and that has alienated, and isolated many by the millions for no other reason than that they were and are of a different skin color. This is the religion of white supremacy. Framing it, white supremacy, in this way allows us to see how devout the nation has been to this anti-secularism as an adherent to a religion, observant of ritual, practice, and liturgy, "whereby dominant groups use state power to affirm and entrench hegemonic identities (white, male, Protestant) as normal, and . . . construe and disparage minority identities as deviant."[5] Therefore, the notion that a liberal democracy requiring a seemingly strict delineation between church and state as untenable and unjust, when considered under the ominous auspices of white supremacist philosophy and expression as both privilege and power, is not a generative or salient thesis. Laborde echoes the sentiments of critical religion theorists, suggesting that "religion is not a natural category of social and ethical experience

---

5. Laborde, *Liberalism's Religion*, 95

... but the category of religion itself, [was] invented and formalized in the process of consolidation of modern states."[6]

However, white supremacy is the religion in America, constitutive of environmental liturgics, and it is highly theocratic in its dimensions:

> Here the dimension of religion that is targeted by the liberal secular state is the theocratic dimension of religion: the claim by churches to rule not only the private but also the public sphere—to enact coercive rules and norms for society as a whole. Instead, the modern state worked to locate religion within the private sphere of individual conscience, voluntary association, and the family—but the precise contours of the boundary between public and private have been fluid and historically contested.[7]

Thus, it is in the tension of this fluidity where what is most cumbersome about viewing white supremacy not as an aberrant machination of evil but as an intentional religion, possessing its own liturgical structure that allows its adherents to either passively or actively participate in it,[8] with dire and deleterious consequences,[9] projects itself twofold. First, a religion as such would not be operable in close environs to the state because it would stipulate the degradation and humiliation of nonwhite citizens, thus being, in effect, racist, limited by that myopic and claustral scope, thereby making the state culpable in the oppression of some of its citizens. Second, in a liberal democratic society, it would reveal the nation that practices such a religion to be confederate with endorsing a religion, which, as I will discuss, is indeed both extant and injurious, and moreover not in keeping with Laborde's innate state secularism.

---

6. Laborde, *Liberalism's Religion*, 171.

7. Laborde, *Liberalism's Religion*, 171.

8. Bakhtin, *Toward a Philosophy*, 41. Passivity of participation is still participation. It is as an actor on stage playing a role that he or she can only play. Though there may be effort supplied to affect the role, the actor ultimately is simply reading lines given to him or her and is only able to play that part, to participate in that rite, "circumscribed by [his or her] occupancy of a particular position, or even of a set of situationally conflicting positions, both in the persisting structure of his society, and also in the rôle structure of the given ritual" (Turner, *Forest of Symbols*, 67). What is more, through this passive activation of role in ritual and rite much damage to others outside the ritual can still be done, for "what is meaningless for an actor playing a specific rôle may well be highly significant for an observer and analyst of the total system" (Turner, *Forest of Symbols*, 67).

9. Russian philosopher Mikhail Bakhtin (*Toward a Philosophy*, 12n15) writes that human beings both actively and passively participate in their being because they are inherently irreplaceable. Therefore, regardless if they know it or not, it is possible to be a participant either directly or indirectly in being a white supremacist.

What is truly challenging about the certainty of white supremacy as religion is that there exists in its thought a reverse anamnesis of sorts occurring today, a misremembering, wherein even scholars deny the existence of deliberate systems of racism and bigotry that aid the systematized religiosity of white supremacy. Therefore, what this essay intends is to promote the naming of liturgies that speak to white supremacy and privilege as America's religion, a religion that has unjustifiably been oft abutted by the state, so that through an ultimate acknowledgment of these liturgies, their adverse results can be curtailed. Hence, this essay will first frame philosophically the argument that America's religion is white supremacy; then it will look at the corrosive societal effects of this religion, particularly the effects representative of economic conditions that led to the eventuation of the senseless killing of Michael Brown (for the treatment of his body and prevenient conditions that led to his death are microcosmic of the systematic religiosity of white supremacy); and lastly it will discuss a probable theological response to a most woefully vacuous religion. For me, the liturgy of this religion had its invocation with the institution of a slavocracy that lasted 246 years in this country and most recently had its benediction in the killing of Michael Brown on August 9, 2014. This will be discussed later.

In *Liberalism's Religion*, Laborde maintains that the state should never alienate the nonreligious by endorsing the votive symbology of religions. In chapter 3, one way she makes this point clear is by stating the deep anthropological experience of African Americans in the country as alienated from descriptions of humanity by being banned from appropriating civic rights, recounting the history of racist litigation in America as an affront to the ontological framework and social mobility of Black people. Nevertheless, by acknowledging certain governmental proclivities that should not exist, Laborde is emphasizing in turn systems that actually are existent and pervasive even to this day. It is these systems that allow for nothing other than deliberate actions of racism today, a fact that Elisabeth Vasko in her book, *Beyond Apathy: A Theology for Bystanders*, ardently denies, suggesting that "most white racism does not result from deliberate or blatant bigotry."[10] However, there is no other way for a person to behave than into which system they act. This is deliberateness by design. This is blatancy by technology. This reliance upon white racial biases is constructive of a racism that has become so routinized it is banal and commonplace and nondescript, thereby permitting a lived experience that borders on the mundane, insists on the ubiquity. This is the essence of racism as ritual, as a system of belief through practice explained as religion.

10. Vasko, *Beyond Apathy*, 66.

On this wise, Slavoj Žižek offers a useful comment, postulating that faith is not from the inward outward but from the outward inward. He believes that what practices a person has are what causes him or her to believe, that that ritual becomes his or her religion through material belief rooted in practice.[11] This is neither the belief, or faith, described in Heb 11, nor is it what Kant "calls 'pragmatic faith,' the arbitrary acceptance, for the purposes of action, of an uncertain proposition." It is the "Practical faith [that] is the condition of entry that every field tacitly imposes, not only by sanctioning and debarring those who would destroy the game, but by so arranging things, in practice, that the operations of selecting and shaping new entrants (rites of passage, examinations, etc.) are such as to obtain from them that undisputed, pre-reflexive, naïve, native compliance with the fundamental presuppositions of the field, which is the very definition of doxa."[12] So that if the secularism of the inclusive state should not support any religious identity, governmentally, or through policy, if this is proven to be so, that America indeed has a religion and that it is white supremacy, it would reveal a great internal schism, at least with regard to the fitness of government to govern, at most with regard to how the government governs, with its espousing of a violent ideology through systematized practice, which becomes legitimized policy, a policy tantamount to religious observance.

This religious identity is forged in the cauldron of American exceptionalism. This is why it becomes cumbersome when in *Beyond Apathy*, Vasko quotes Kelly Brown Douglas and her book *Stand Your Ground: Black Bodies and the Justice of God,* yet is still not able to connect white American exceptionalism with the notion of the deliberate actions of racism. This assumption is challenging in the Vasko text because through it she never really delves deeply into the problem of mythos qua mythos apropos of European and American imperial conquest. She makes the comment: "In the United States, whiteness is marked by the presumption of dominance and entitlement," yet she does not trace its origin. Moreover, she makes statements like: "Contrary to popular belief, most white racism does not result from deliberate or blatant bigotry," when the entire system in which the actors play on stage (theatre too being a kind of ritual) is and has been predicated by deliberate and blatant bigotry. It is important to note this because it imputes an intentionality that is real, tangible, appreciable, and consequent. This is important because white privilege extends from white supremacy, which lends itself to the consciousness of American selfhood, extending from a narratology of racial primacy and superiority that has the existential

---

11. Pound, *Žižek*, 55.
12. Bourdieu, *Logic of Practice*, 68.

force of historicity on its side. She quotes from Kelly Brown Douglas's necessary book *Stand Your Ground* but neglects to lift out the phraseology most poignant to white supremacy's striking genesis as evinced through the narrativity and mythos of the effusive Tacitus work *Germania* (c. 98 CE). Douglas's book is an interrogation of the cultural normatives that engendered the atmosphere for Trayvon Martin's murder (similar to those that created the infrastructure that led to Michael Brown's killing), maintaining that the "seeds [that allowed a Stand Your Ground law] were planted well before the founding of America [and these] seeds produced a myth of racial superiority that both determined America's founding and defined its identity."[13] Douglas contends that this mythos "gave way to America's grand narrative of Anglo-Saxon exceptionalism."[14] It is this same narratology, one of divine election, one of holy importance, one of manifest destiny, that animated the corpus of American solipsistic personhood and predicated its inclination towards and inculcation of privilege. Here is her recounting of Tacitus from the section of her book entitled "The Making of the Anglo-Saxon Myth":

> In *Germania* Tacitus provides a meticulous portrait, based on others' writings and observations, of the Germanic tribes who fended off Rome's first century empire-building agenda. He identifies the tribes as an "aboriginal" people "free from all taint of intermarriages." They are, he says, "a distinct unmixed race, like none but themselves," with "fierce blue eyes, red hair, huge frames." Tacitus commended these Germans for their bravery and strong moral character. "No one in Germany," he explained, "laughs at vice." He went on to say that for these Germans "good [moral] habits" were more effectual than "good laws."[15]

The consequences of insistence certainly abound here. Notice the insistence upon the high moral superiority of these Germanic peoples with motility towards it being natural, immanent, and inherent. What is more is the insistence upon them being an "unmixed race," signaling the construction of a foundation of genetic purity being condign with morality and rightness. To wit, these people are the best people and there are none liken unto them under the heavens. What is most provocative here is not only what the historian Tacitus wrote, but also the conspicuousness upon the power of narrative to compel things to exist. No wonder his *Germania*, written even as far back as year 98, has been called "one of the most dangerous books ever written."[16] Vasko suggests that moral apathy is concomitant with white

13. Douglas, *Stand Your Ground*, 13.
14. Douglas, *Stand Your Ground*, 40.
15. Douglas, *Stand Your Ground*, 5.
16. Krebs, *Most Dangerous Book*, 16.

privilege and that it is a deficit to American theologizing in general, and she rightly connects the problematics to masculinist Christian theology, connecting the lynching culture of postbellum America with the crucifixion of Jesus and how "Christianity's classical atonement tradition [mitigated that] ... a crowd that lynches, therefore, would not immediately repulse such a God. A God that sanctions a human sacrifice as brutal as crucifixion can serve as a divine ally for those who make such a sacrifice—even a sacrifice as horrific as lynching."[17] But you do not have a lynching, or a killing of an unarmed Black man, unless the state abets these killings. As a God who did not spare his own son would seem to sanction the extrajudicial slaying of persons, so too would a state whose religion is white supremacy. Perhaps the problem that these killings perdure is that the government has not become aware that they are indeed participant and culpable in a state-sanctioned religion that is racist to its core.

Žižek, in his discussion of the materiality of belief evinced as religious practice, suggests:

> Religious belief... is not merely, or even primarily, an inner conviction; but the Church is an institution and its rituals (prayers, baptism, confirmation, confession ... which far from being a mere secondary externalization of the inner belief, stands for the very mechanism that generates it.[18]

Though one may not believe that one is racist, though the government itself may not believe itself to be racist, the ritualistic rigor with which it has and continues to enact certain policies (the redlining of housing districts, the developing of voter suppression laws [both archaic and modern], et al.) chooses a racist distinction for both the self and the state. Moreover, even if one does not readily subscribe to racist policy overtly, in substance, by being confederate in systems governmentally that disenfranchise/d and marginalize/d some while exalting others, i.e., slavery, lynching, Jim Crow, the prison industrial complex, and voter suppression, there is a keeping with past commitments to racialized oppression that perpetuates itself. This is what Pierre Bourdieu (borrowed from Eric Havelock) calls *practical mimesis*:

> A practical mimesis ... has nothing in common with an imitation that would presuppose a conscious effort to reproduce a gesture, an utterance or an object explicitly constituted as a model ... [instead,] the process of reproduction [takes] place

---

17. Douglas, *What's Faith Got to Do*, 72.
18. Žižek, *Žižek Reader*, 65–66.

below the level of consciousness, expression and the reflexive distance which these presuppose . . . . What is "learned by the body" is not something that one has, like knowledge that can be brandished, but something that one is.[19]

It is here that Martha Nussbaum in her book *The Monarchy of Fear: A Philosopher Looks at Our Political Crisis* begins to language the specific racist aggressions extant in the observed Laborde system of political description, of which Vasko, quoting Massingale,[20] suggests that there is little deliberateness and blatancy, calling this space a monarchy of fear that is filled with disgust. Yet, this is the phenomenon that permits the white racist and white supremacist policy to exist, "fueling what psychologists call 'implicit bias'—bias that shows up on empirical tests, even though the biased person is not aware of having it."[21] This is what allows the white racist to avoid complicity of recognition of action, because he or she is simply acting out what has been done before him or her in a highly ritualized system tantamount to a religion in the "practical world that is constituted in the relationship with the *habitus* [a product of history, [producing] individual and collective practices—*more* history—in accordance with the schemes generated by history[22]], acting as a system of cognitive and motivating structures . . . a world of already realized ends—procedures to follow, paths to take—and of objects endowed with a 'permanent teleological character,' in Husserl's phrase, tools or *institutions*."[23] It is what is learned in the body, which Bourdieu likens to a game:

> The earlier a player enters . . . the less aware of the associated learning (the limiting case being, of course, that of someone born into, born with the game), the greater is his ignorance of all that is tacitly granted through his investment in the field and his interest in its very existence and perpetuation and in everything that is played for in it, and his unawareness of the

---

19. Bourdieu, *Logic of Practice*, 73.

20. Vasko, *Beyond Apathy*, 32.

21. Nussbaum, *Monarchy of Fear*, 109.

22. Bourdieu, *Logic of Practice*, 54. Here is a more exhaustive definition of *habitus* from Bourdieu's book relative to how it fits into my idea of white supremacy as ritualized/religious practice: "The *habitus* is the principle of a selective perception of the indices tending to confirm and reinforce it rather than transform it, a matrix generating responses adapted in advance to all objective conditions identical to or homologous with the (past) conditions of its production; it adjusts itself to a probable future which it anticipates and helps to bring about because it reads it directly in the present of the presumed world, the only one it can ever know" (64).

23. Bourdieu, *Logic of Practice*, 53. Italics added.

unthought presuppositions that the game produces and endlessly reproduces, thereby reproducing the conditions of its own perpetuation.[24]

It is the belief system that one inhabits, and dutifully so, daily. This is why it is so easy for white people to live into white supremacy, because they have no inkling that they are in fact doing so (and through their actions they reinforce and enliven its structures and substructures); they simply mimic behaviors that were generated generationally long before they came to exist. Moreover, belief (as Žižek reads Pascal) arises in the metaxological realm, between the participant in the religion (white racists) and the ritual itself (racism as a religion). One does not have to admit that one is racist, because one's racist actions believe for oneself, no different than rituals believing on the behalf of the participant of a religion, a point that Bourdieu affirms:

> In contrast to logic, a mode of thought that works by making explicit the work of thought, practice excludes all formal concerns. Reflexive attention to action itself, when it occurs (almost invariably only when the automatism has broken down), remains subordinate to the pursuit of the result and to the search (not necessarily perceived in this way) for maximum effectiveness of the effort expended. So it has nothing in common with the aim of explaining how the result has been achieved, still less of seeking to understand (for understanding's sake) the logic of practice, which flouts logical logic.[25]

If we take Bourdieu here at face value, it can be broadly construed that practice, particularly that of ritual or rite, is not only what believes *on behalf* of a person, according to Žižek's reading, but is done without any inherent or innate system of logics of its own. Thus, it is both unthinking and unlearned, even of its own history, of its own origin, or of its own purpose for being carried out. Ritual just continues as it is, as it has been for years, for decades, for centuries. And this longevity is but a symptom of its functionality, that is, how it can conceal its religiosity and free it from all mystification and magics, restoring "its reason and raison d'être, without converting it into a logical construction or spiritual exercise:"[26]

> To give an idea of the complexity of this network of circuits of circular causality, by the material conditions apprehended by agents endowed with schemes of perception that are themselves

---

24. Bourdieu, *Logic of Practice*, 67.
25. Bourdieu, *Logic of Practice*, 91.
26. Bourdieu, *Logic of Practice*, 97.

determined, negatively at least, by these conditions (translated into a particular form of the relations of production), it is sufficient to point out that one of the functions of rites—especially those accompanying marriage, ploughing or harvesting—is to overcome in practice the specifically ritual contradiction which the ritual taxonomy sets up by dividing the world into contrary principles and by causing the acts most indispensable to the survival of the group to appear as acts of sacrilegious violence.[27]

A central, unifying tenet of ritual as practice is that it embeds itself into a milieu, making the religiosity of the ritual to appear not to be what it is. To maintain the practice and to obscure its harms is what ritual often does, and this explains the challenges in effectively confronting the ritualized religion of white supremacy.

This religion of white supremacy was established with its own liturgics long ago: slavery was really a kind of invocation, an opening prayer or hymn, that fervently adumbrated the hopes and dreams of a people who wished to degrade a certain few so that they would be able to reap the generational benefits of free labor—no cupidity hidden, no brutality spared, no whip uncracked. And this liturgics provided the optics through which the lectionary of white racist policy today is meted out, as I shall uncover, looking at the tragic events in Ferguson, Missouri, in 2014, as a microcosmic example of the American state. In this discourse, it began with the shooting of Michael Brown and how his body lay there treated with the same respect that one would grant a furtive animal. Decomposing in the sun under waves of that summer swelter was not only that young man's life, all that he was and all that he ever would be, but also the moral composition of the nation. For, in those moments austere, when the Black body rotted openly, so too the community that brought the young man to adulthood corrupted, having to witness such inexplicably quick and lasting barbarity. There have been scholars who have written about the conditions that led to the young man's killing and the effects of that killing, many like George Lipsitz, who wrote in the University of Minnesota Press in the article "From *Plessy* to Ferguson," that there is a thread that runs direct from the consequential civil case to the conditions that permitted Michael Brown's killing by Officer Darren Wilson, who acted as nothing less than a participant in the liturgical codification that he inherited. Lipsitz cites redlining in housing, segregation of schools, and workplace discriminatory practices as factors that engendered an atmosphere that led to Brown's death, practices that were all in the ritualistic observation of America's true religion. But this must come later.

27. Bourdieu, *Logic of Practice*, 97.

In *Beyond Ontological Blackness: An Essay on African American Religious and Cultural Criticism*, Victor Anderson seeks a new way of defining what it means to be Black in America. In his thesis, he forsakes all categorical racial descriptions of Blackness, and seeks ardently to abscond the traditionalism of ontological mores conducive to elucidating what it means to be Black. Observing that for decades Blackness as an ethos of being has oft been substantiated by its perceived epic and intrinsic struggle against white supremacy, he stipulates in a logic of reductio ad absurdum that this creates an ontology that is strictly limiting and myopic in its scope and scale.

> Existentially, the new Black being remains bound by whiteness. Politically, it remains unfulfilled because Blackness is ontologically defined as the experience of suffering and survival.[28]

For Anderson, Blackness as an identity should not seek to be apologist after David Walker, W. E. B. Du Bois, Booker T. Washington, and Marcus Garvey, nor should it be heroic after Apollo, but should be Nietzschean in its grotesquerie, afforded every convulation and complication assigned to all other realms of humanity on the planet. Then and only then can a new being of Blackness emerge, one that is not monumental or monolithic but pluralistic and heteronormative in a redemptive and generative way.

Anderson rejects all methods of ascribing a categorical disposition of Black identity. Therefore, it is not a liberative way for Black people to look at themselves through the lens of category about race—it is essentializing, editorializing, monumentalizing, and bleak. Hence, this is not my argument, that Black people view themselves in this way. My contention, rather, is that this is the way white people view Black people. I realize what I design is not to describe Blackness, because Black people are organically coming into what and who they are to be in this country. They do not need my help with that. There is no threat to Blackness by way of a faulty, fallacious, or listless self-prescribed ontology. Rather the greatest threat to Black ontology has always been white ontology. It is the phenomenology of white ontology that needs to be affected. This work centers on how ontological whiteness, abetted by structures of power and privilege, specifically the governmental abetting white supremacy as religion, has not been allowed to be undone since the established parameters of a trichotomy of signs—the chain (icon), the lynching tree (index), and Jim Crow (symbol)—and, because of this, white people have been able to live into a system of privilege with ease and dexterity, causing further acts of oppressive violence against Black people, my contention being that the soon to be mentioned statistical data are

---

28 Anderson, *Beyond Ontological Blackness*, 93.

proclivities that could be no other way but consequent of the iconicity of the Black person's existentialism. It will consequently be my work to abolish this trichotomy, which lends itself to the formation of white privilege and racist proclivity, and establish a redemptive theology in response to it.

It all starts with the sign. This is firstness; this is the initial sense, the quality (quale) associated with the subject, called the *icon*. Regarding historicity (always), for the Black person regarding citizenship, the initial sign, the icon in this trichotomy of signs is the *chain*;[29] for in it is the feeling, the sense of abject servitude. She was brought here in chains, her first station was enchained, relegated to a posture of *subservience*; thus, naturally this, the chain, must serve as the sign to her ontological indexicality (that which points to her being) in this trichotomy of signs. Charles Sanders Peirce maintained that the icon is that which predicates the trichotomy of semiotics. If the icon of the Black person is the chain, how could this ever bode well for her in the American context? How much further can the Black person deign to mobilize from this position, for in the chain is the sense, the feeling, the quality of hopelessness, or degradation, or subservience to a powerful elite?

The next natural motility for the Black person in America, moving from the icon, informed by it, is the *index*, which represents secondness, which represents the tangibility, that which is rooted in reality, that which emerges from the icon and that has immutable consequences. In this case, the index is the *noose*. The difference between the chain and the noose is condign with the lynching tree, for in those lynchings are the souls of innocent lives lost with statistical rigor that is tangible, as are its ramifications today. James Hal Cone in his *The Cross and the Lynching Tree* explains that during slavery there were no lynchings as praxis because the slave owner would not destroy his own property; however after slavery, starting particularly after Reconstruction had its day of futility, there began the practice of lynching as a way to remind the formerly enslaved and their progeny of their continued place of subjugation as second-class citizens, "free" or not.[30] Therefore, here in the noose, hung on the lynching tree, we find that the Black person in America has been relegated physically with a view to being relegated systemically politically in the thirdness of this trichotomy of signs, the *symbol*.

The symbol, which represents thirdness, which is constitutive and consequent of all the significations consequent of the icon, as pointed out by the index, in this line of reasoning is *Jim Crow*. This is because Jim Crow

---

29. Peirce, "On a New List of Categories."
30. Cone, *Cross and Lynching Tree*, 132.

generated policies that were but a foretaste for the societal strictures that still pervade to the present time. In the symbol there is universality—and in a quite literal sense Jim Crow has created an emanated universe within which the Black person still lives and moves and has its being today, as postulated by Michelle Alexander in her book, *The New Jim Crow: Mass Incarceration in the Age of Colorblindness*. For example, due to the white supremacist mentality concomitant with market morality, the outsourcing of jobs and technological advancements open only to those highly educated persons, Black men were deindustrialized from 1970 to 1987, from 70 percent to 28 percent, this leading to radical poverty in urban communities.[31] This economic shutting out led to the pursuit of monies illegally through the sales of crack cocaine and marijuana among Black men. But while white men are seven times more likely to possess crack, white students are seven times more likely to use powder cocaine than Black students,[32] and equally likely to use and possess marijuana (with marijuana-related arrests being responsible for 80 percent of all arrests in the 1990s),[33] Black people are five times more likely to be imprisoned. 80 to 90 percent of all drug offenders sent to prison are Black,[34] so that by 2006 one out of fourteen Black men were behind bars.[35]

In 1987, during the vestiges of the Reagan administration, the funding for drug abuse centers nationwide dropped from 274 million to 57 million and for education from 14 million to 3 million.[36] In 1994, under Black people's second favorite white president, Bill Clinton, 17 billion dollars was removed from public housing initiatives, a drop of 61 percent, while 19 billion dollars went toward the construction of new prisons, a boon of 171 percent,[37] hastening the increase in the number of people caught in Michel Foucault's "carceral circle" and the creation of what Michelle Alexander calls a racial "under-caste."

This is the legacy of the *icon*, the chain. It is in these social environs that Michael Brown was born, came of age, and was killed, in a society that conferred upon him the designation of other, of alterity, of erasure, and of non-citizenship, when he, according to American law, had all the rights and privileges of citizenship; yet his body was treated as a nonentity. These are

---

31. Alexander, *New Jim Crow*, 50–51.
32. Alexander, *New Jim Crow*, 99.
33. Alexander, *New Jim Crow*, 99 and 60.
34. Alexander, *New Jim Crow*, 98.
35. Alexander, *New Jim Crow*, 100.
36. Alexander, *New Jim Crow*, 50–51.
37. Alexander, *New Jim Crow*, 57.

the parameters of being that are not observed by Blackness but by whiteness in America as it participates both actively and passively in the religion of white supremacy.

Homer Plessy thought he could elude this trichotomy ascribed to him by whiteness and live into being white. He did not care too much about the plight of Black people in America; he simply thought that reasonably he, a light-skinned Black man, who could pass for white, "whose ancestry was seven-eighths white,"[38] should be able to be participant in the religion of white supremacy, only to find that the doors of the church were not opened to him. Plessy's argument before the supreme court justices in the landmark *Plessy v. Ferguson* was that he should by virtue of his near-white appearance be able to inhabit the religious ecology of white supremacy and board the segregated railroad cars in Louisiana. The result of this man's desire to adhere to a religion that only white people can practice was disastrous for Black people across the country as the disseminated verdict ruled that it is constitutional for Black people to live in a society where they must remain separated from whiteness, but somehow still be considered equal. To the hypocrisy of this concept Laborde writes, elucidating why it is difficult for state and religion to coincide:

> By analogy, U.S. segregation laws disparaged African Americans, not because they offended African American culture and ways of life, but because they construed blackness as a negative ascriptive identity, a marker of subordination and inferiority. What the ban on civic disparagement focuses on are those dimensions of the socially constructed meanings of religion that structurally resemble other suspect categories of oppression and domination, such as race.[39]

Being separate would never allow equality of Blackness in the eyes of whiteness in America, a point that even the one dissenting vote by Judge Henry Billings Brown in the watershed decision revealed. As a good white person, the lone dissenter, Brown, a devout participant in the religion of white supremacy, would affirm its power, even in a moment of self-aggrandizing righteousness:

> The white race deems itself to be the dominant race in this country. And so it is in prestige, in achievements, in education, in wealth and in power. So, I doubt not, it will continue to be for all

---

38. Lipsitz, "From *Plessy* to Ferguson," 40.
39. Laborde, *Liberalism's Religion*, 96.

time if it remains true to its great heritage and holds fast to the principles of constitutional liberty.[40]

This separateness bespeaks the white supremacist concept of otherness that endures even unto this day. For from the *Plessy* decision came the disjointed and derelict housing practices in Missouri that created the atmosphere for Michael Brown's killing, for "Be it by design, accident, or benign neglect, the fuse that led to the explosion in Ferguson was lit in St. Louis more than 60 years ago."[41] Michael Brown would not have even been on Canfield Drive in the suburb of Ferguson, Missouri, if it had not been for the failure of the Pruitt-Igoe.

Pruitt-Igoe was a housing complex in St. Louis that was funded by the United States Housing Act of 1949. The act funded cities monies to "clear slums, redevelop urban space, and build affordable housing" for underprivileged and underserved residents. The acme of this "housing experiment" was found in the Pruitt-Igoe complex, which was comprised of "thirty-three towers that rose eleven stories high."[42] It was a bastion, a veritable monument to governmental architectural and economic might, but when it failed it became a perceived testament to its tenants' (mainly poor Black persons) inferiority, though for many of them it seemed "an oasis in a desert."[43] These tenants were made to suffer under conditions that exploited their poverty, "making their rent and food more expensive than the mortgages and groceries paid by suburban whites,"[44] (a trend that has always existed in Black communities, with a report in 2013 revealing that one in eight poor renting families nationwide were unable to pay all of their rent)[45] and their perceived failure to respond triumphally to shoddy construction and exorbitantly escalating rent costs became "a symbol for Black pathology and a catalyst for the consolidation of white power, a consolidation achieved through zoning laws, among other things, that would prevent the construction of other Pruitt-Igoes and protect the racial integrity of white suburbs."[46] The failure of Pruitt-Igoe, as characterized by Katharine G. Bristol, was a result of "institutionalized economic and racial oppression" and it is what pushed Black people from the housing tenement to the largely white suburbs of St. Louis, such as Normandy, Jennings, Wellston, Bellefontaine Neighbors,

40. Lipsitz, "From *Plessy* to Ferguson," 128.
41. Ferguson, "Michael Brown, Ferguson," 140.
42. Ferguson, "Michael Brown, Ferguson," 140.
43. Ferguson, "Michael Brown, Ferguson," 140–41.
44. Ferguson, "Michael Brown, Ferguson," 141.
45. Desmond, *Evicted*, 5.
46. Ferguson, "Michael Brown, Ferguson," 141.

and Ferguson. This Black flight caused white fright, which, in turn, predicated white flight in which the former white residents of those areas "moved further north but retained their control of law enforcement and municipal government in those areas," which propounded the concrescence of "white authority and myths of Black inferiority,"[47] stemming from the recent perceived cultural failure of Pruitt-Igoe.

And it is in this environment that Michael Brown was forced to exist, which exposed him to what Nussbaum calls the monarchy of fear, in which she posits perhaps it would be fruitful for white people, and those members of society who have been otherized and marginalized by whiteness, to live together, to inhabit the same environs, to be exposed to one another as a means of ending white supremacy. This is a slightly naïve viewpoint that stipulates the benevolence of whiteness, since whiteness sits in the position of privilege and prestige in American society. For example, Nussbaum suggests that it would be best to have the marginalized people to live with the people in privilege, that the races should be exposed to one another on a frequent basis, and that by doing so, it would help to rectify the relations between them, citing her own analysis that "disgust feeds on fantasies of the other, and sharing a common daily life is the best way to explode these fantasies."[48] However, this view completely neglects the sordid histories of white and Black Americans who have shared spaces on different occasions with disastrous results. I am reminded specifically of the Draft Riots of 1863, in which Irish men and women ravaged the streets of Manhattan, destroying property, and killing Black people, fetishizing their body parts. The Irish, who immigrated from Ireland due to the potato famine of 1851, came to the United States in search of a new life, one wherein they could provide for their families and subsist bountifully away from food scarcity. Once arrived, they were prejudicially treated by the more Germanic whites, who did not consider the Irish white in the way that they were white, but slightly subhuman. Thus, they were relegated, similarly to how the Black people were relegated, to a second-rate citizenship, even made to inhabit the same living space as Black people, particularly in New York City. The Irish were drafted at a high rate and thus killed at a high rate in the bloodiest war ever for American soldiers. Though the Irish shared community with Black people each day, it could not prevent them from destroying Black life and Black property, , causing a riot and forcing the survivors of the riot to deal (for years to come) with the humiliation of being a Black resident on the

---

47. Ferguson, "Michael Brown, Ferguson," 141.
48. Nussbaum, *Monarchy of Fear*, 112.

Lower East Side.[49] Moreover, this thinking resists the reality that white identity is so tied to power that any perceived loss of that power will throw (and has thrown) whiteness into an existential crisis. But one does not simply end white supremacy, because it is not a philosophical construct; it is a religion that has a devout adherent populace of no mean size. Therefore, until there is a mass exodus from this religion into a more generative system that is inclusive, or no system at all, but a political way of being that is just and liberating, holding the powerful to account, then the pernicious acts of white supremacy will continue to persist throughout time.

The failure of Pruitt-Igoe (which was eventually demolished in 1972) is what catapulted Michaelf Brown, as well as many other Black people, towards Ferguson, and they are what hurtled him tragically towards Canfield Drive and to be shot six times, killed by an officer who had sworn to protect him, his rights, his liberties, his pursuit of happiness, his body left humiliated there in the middle of the street for over four hours. Darren Wilson and Michael Brown were only four years apart in age and they were the same height, both 6'4", though Wilson, to justify his shooting of Brown, would go on to describe the teen as a "demon" and "Hulk Hogan-like."[50] The only appreciable characteristic that separated the two young men was that, while Michael Brown was Black, Darren Wilson is white. This is what allowed Officer Wilson to live into the ecology that is white supremacy as the national religion; this is what enabled him to, within ninety seconds of arriving to confront Michael Brown and Dorian Johnson in the street, shoot Brown six times, killing him, though Wilson had originally been called to Canfield Drive in response to a baby having breathing problems;[51] this is what allowed "the police chain of command to permit Officer Wilson to go into hiding without being questioned or having to file a comprehensive written report explaining the shooting"; this is what allowed the "Ferguson Police Chief Thomas Jackson to release a video to the press in an effort to smear the reputation of the deceased Brown"; this is what allowed "the chief to lie that he was required to release the video because of a Freedom of Information Act request when in fact none had been filed"; this is what allowed "Ferguson and county police officers to attack demonstrators and reporters"; this is what allowed "the county prosecutor [to turn] the grand jury process into an exercise in exculpating Officer Wilson and [mount] a public relations campaign on his behalf by repeatedly leaking secret testimony"; this is what allowed "the prosecutorial team [to instruct] the grand jury

---

49. Burns, *New York*.
50. Bouie, "Michael Brown," para. 3.
51. Patrick, "Darren Wilson's Radio Calls."

to decide Wilson's culpability on the basis of a statute they knew had been declared unconstitutional"; this is what allowed "white people with no real factual knowledge about the incident [to collect] more than $500,000 from sympathizers for a fund for Officer Wilson (who had been charged with no crime and made no appeal for a legal defense fund)";[52] this is what allowed the verdict in the eventual Brown/Wilson case to result in a wrongful death lawsuit that was settled out of court—a clear dearth of governmental secularism conducive to an abetted religion. This is no mere monarchy of fear, as has been supposed; this is a deliberate system of systems in which ritual becomes practice, practice becomes faith, faith becomes God, and the dreadful and dolorous liturgy of white supremacy ambles on. If slavery was an invocation, then the lynching tree was a sermon, reminding the newly enfranchised Black citizens that, though white people had no control over their bodies, they still could deign to control their minds by instilling in them terror; Jim Crow was the Eucharist, around which white bodies can fellowship around the subjugation, animalization, and essentialization of Blackness in America; the killing of Michael Brown, as well as the killings of unarmed Black people across the nation, enumerated with unspeakable frequency, is a benediction—a good saying, to whites only, of a ritual well practiced and a job well done, that they are in right standing with their faith, their tradition, their religion, and their God. Michael Brown, though ostensibly an American citizen, was not able to be participant in this liturgy of supremacy and privilege simply because he was Black; yet, Darren Wilson was enabled to do so, innately and instinctively, through practical mimesis, and through the bodily and embodied learning of ritual, namely the ritual of the state's regulated and enforced religion of white supremacy.

In *The Punitive Society*, Foucault discloses that delinquency is tethered to carcerality.[53] By this he means that there is a need within incarceration for delinquency, the committing of a crime, that unless crime is committed, the carceral or prison as industry cannot subsist. The two desperately need each other to survive. Further is the problem that in the United States there are on average some over 2 million persons in the armed forces (active and in reserve);[54] yet there are some 6.9 million persons subjugated in the corrections population today—2.2 million people incarcerated and 4.75 million on probation or parole—[55] 34 percent of whom are Black,[56] suggesting that

52. Lipsitz, "From *Plessy* to Ferguson," 125.
53. Foucault, *Ethics*, 25–26.
54. Lai et al., "Is America's Military Big Enough?" para. 10.
55. Kaeble and Glaze, "Correctional Populations."
56. NAACP, *Criminal Justice Fact Sheet*.

America, a nation that spends just over half a trillion dollars on defense (more than any country in the world) cares more about penalizing people than protecting them. Thus, this immuring that Du Bois felt as a child and expressed in 1903, has become actualized through the imprisonment of Black bodies, creating the atmosphere for the Michael Brown killing in what Foucault called the carceral state, or the punitive society. These are the results of the seeds sown during the time of the chain, the *icon*, the quality of what was to be. This is the fulfillment of the denial of Blackness in America. So that when Darren Wilson responded with wildcat visceraility, he did so not as a unique actor, he did so in the only way that made sense to him as an executor of a carceral state steeped in deafening semiotics.

For the Black person, America is a cradle of violence—it has acted apathetically to secure her complete liberation, it has hastened her brutalization, it has mocked at her disenfranchisement, it has thwarted her overtures towards parity, it has winked at her sufferings throughout its history of aggrandizing, self-congratulating ascendancy. But this violence is a result of her, the Black person, not being seen as equal, not truly being a citizen, *ever*, and still never. And this is with lasting effect. And this is the goal of the spiritual striving, to rout what Du Bois once justly posited as the problem of the twentieth century, "the problem of the color-line." It is also the problem of the twenty-first century, and, if this problem is not dealt with right now, it will lead to many more cases such as Michael Brown, who because of his Blackness had to live above reproach, who because of his Blackness was not allowed to take up too much space, who because of his Blackness was animalized, killed like a dirty dog in the street. And then it will be the problem of this century and all other centuries. And the trauma will continue.

It is this phenomenon that William Cavanaugh explores in *Torture and Eucharist: Theology, Politics, and the Body of Christ*. In the book, torture is used to rob the tortured of their time, rather to have imparted the time of the torturer, the torturer's language, the torturer's universe of discourse, the torturer's self into the tortured over the course of time. The torturer would make, specifically in Chile under the Pinochet regime, the tortured confess to crimes they had not committed, giving the victims "ideas which conform to the torturer's reality [where] the tortured are made to speak the words of the regime, to replace their own reality with that of the state."[57] This is what Cavanaugh means by "the disappeared." The tortured are kept over time (even after being tortured) so that they are killed in the minds of others in their community, disrupting the fabric of society to fit the needs

---

57. Cavanaugh, *Torture and Eucharist*, 30.

of the torturers.[58] The disappeared are not only those whose demise was sanctioned by the state through the act of torture (and subsequent disposal of their bodies) but those that were allowed to remain alive but were not who they once were due to the unusual punishment that they endured. They are shadows of who they used to be. Trauma is consequent of torture, and the inhumanity of the torture is not just in the violence perpetrated upon the victims of torture but the intent behind the torture. If we look at the violence visited constantly upon the Black population of America, we can see that the trauma visited upon them is tantamount to torture. They are no longer themselves (not in an ontological way but in a functional way) but something other, something afeared, something apprehensive, something skeptical, a being not fully integrated into the fabric of the society that they inhabit, non-citizens.

The bottom line is this: in America, Black people make up only 13 percent of the populace but are the victims of 39 percent of the deaths by police while not attacking;[59] though Black people only use drugs 1 percent more than their white counterparts, 547 more of Black people are arrested for drug use than white people, among 100,000 residents annually;[60] Black people are imprisoned five times more than white people; Black people have net values significantly lower than white people, where, in Boston alone, while white households have an average net worth of 247,500 dollars, Black households have a total net worth of *eight* dollars;[61] Black women on average make only 61 cents for every dollar a white man makes;[62] Black babies in the U.S. are twice as likely to die before their first birthday as white babies; Black mothers are three to four times more likely to die from pregnancy-related causes than white women;[63] Black students in Arkansas are five times more likely to be suspended than white students, and 338 percent more likely to be suspended than white students in Minnesota.[64] These statistical data are proclivities that could be no other way consequent of the iconicity of the Black person's existentialist tie to the icon of the chain and America's benighted selfhood relative to its self-deception as being exceptional. These things could be no other way and will be no other way as long as America

---

58. Cavanaugh, *Torture and Eucharist*, 30.
59. Lopez, "There Are Huge Racial Disparities," para. 1.
60. Lopez, "There Are Huge Racial Disparities," para. 3.
61. "That was no typo: The median net worth of black Bostonians really is $8" (Johnson, "Boston. Racism").
62. Nelson, "Black Women and the Pay Gap," para. 1.
63. Neely, *Black Babies Twice as Likely*, para. 1.
64. Green, "Why Are Black Students Punished," para. 2.

refuses to be self-appraising in a productive and amenable way, constructing a theology of self-redemption.

Foucault quotes Seneca's stoic philosophy of apprehension and betterment of self, a philosophy contemporaneous with Paul's ecclesiology, suggesting that there are three modes of self-actualization that a person must undertake to be fulfilled in what life s/he desires to live. First, for the person to be actualized, there must be understood the *importance of listening*, that "the disciple must at first keep silent and listen." (I will speak more on this later.) Second, for the person to be actualized, there must be insistence on the *importance, too, of writing*, "taking notes on the readings, conversations, and reflections that one hears or has or does, ... which must be reread from time to time in order to reactualize what they contain." Third, and for this portion of discourse the most significant, is the persistence of the *importance of habitual self-reflection*, to "commit to memory the things that one has learned, ... to come back inside oneself and examine the 'riches' that one has deposited there."[65] This point is most significant because it questions the person's rigor with regard to how intentionally scrutinizing s/he is, needing the habituation of consideration of creedal deeds, praxes, operations, policies that constitute her or his very being. Thus, if America is truly a democratic nation, where is the practical, structural evidence of this substance of this selfhood? Seneca reveals there is the need for the person to consider her or his actions before s/he can be considered a fully realized, actualized, and fulfilled person. Yet, America never has lived into a model of selfhood consistent with democracy. He, America (and this masculine first-person singular pronoun is intentionally used because the nation was designed by men to benefit particularly land-owning white men), has not lived into what he has claimed for himself; his actions are inconsistent with how he narrativizes himself and are self-deceptive, and it is this self-deception that will prevent him from adopting change. (There will be more on this later.) In his *Existentialism Is a Humanism*, Jean-Paul Sartre pronounces perhaps his most famous theory, "Existence precedes essence."[66] The thought here is that one is born surrounded by options and that one does not become who one shall be until one chooses from the options. In short, a person is revealed through the election of her choices. America as a self has actualized a self that is wholly antithetical to what it professes to be—a deeply just, lawful, free democratic republic society, where all peoples may come and pursue happiness.

---

65. Foucault, *Ethics*, 101.
66. Steven Crowell, "Existentialism"

Thus, theologically, I indict the limitations of Black citizenship in the wake of the Brown shooting, using as a springboard for this leg of discourse Acts 22:24–29:

> The tribune directed that he was to be brought into the barracks, and ordered him to be examined by flogging, to find out the reason for this outcry against him. But when they had tied him up with thongs, Paul said to the centurion who was standing by, "Is it legal for you to flog a Roman citizen who is uncondemned?" When the centurion heard that, he went to the tribune and said to him, "What are you about to do? This man is a Roman citizen." The tribune came and asked Paul, "Tell me, are you a Roman citizen?" And he said, "Yes." The tribune answered, "It cost me a large sum of money to get my citizenship." Paul said, "But I was born a citizen. Those who were about to interrogate him withdrew immediately. The commander himself was alarmed when he realized that he had put Paul, a Roman citizen, in chains.[67]

Consequently, the apostle Paul, Greek by heritage, Jew by culture, was a citizen of Rome and could say circa 60–65 CE in the words of Cicero from back in 70 BCE "Civis romanus sum"—"I am a Roman citizen." And this statement carried so much weight that the centurions quaked at the very thought of apprehending any quiver of his flesh or detaining his personhood without cause. Note that the personhood of the state respected the citizenship, that inimitable relationship to the individual it governs, as a person. Moreover, perhaps if America would view himself on these terms, the terms of personhood, his dealings with persons would be more benevolent, more magnanimous, more just. However, the problem here remains: if America does not view the Black being as a citizen, he will no doubt fail to see her as a person. This neglecting the Black person as a citizen with apparent, fully recognizable rights is but a result of the state-funded and abetted religion of white supremacy.

Nevertheless, I contend that if even in the Roman Empire (an imperious kingdom world-renowned for its brutality and austerity of governance, a conglomerate of nations that perfected a mode of execution invented by the Persians, called crucifixion) could afford a citizen certain visibly unalienable accommodations to exist as a denizen with dignity, how much more should the United States of America have allowed Michael Brown juridical latitude with regard to his woefully poorly executed apprehension and the inhumane handling of his body thereafter? Paul could say not only

---

67. Acts 22:24–29 NRSV.

can you not summarily execute me in the street, but you cannot even touch me without first bringing me before Caesar or a local magistrate. I identify Darren Wilson not as an aberrant actor but as a paragon of a broken system of government, a system that places no value on Black lives. God, for the American majority, is tantamount to whiteness, and whiteness is tantamount to domination and privilege.

Politically, this is a savage critique upon a nation that so dearly grabs with both hands (*ultraque manu*), clings to (*adfigere*), and has made indispensable of its national identity (*partem sui facere*)[68] the notion that it is indeed a state that constitutionally seeks justice. The apostle Paul could say that as a Roman citizen he was beyond apprehension without just cause, which speaks to how his body should be treated. His body, Paul's, could not be touched, lest those culpable be punished, and this under the dictatorship of the mad emperor Nero. This is the Roman Empire, a collective of nations under one headship of authority that did not claim to be Christian, that did not claim to be the land of the free and the home of the brave, that was not founded by deists or settled by folk seeking religious freedom to worship specifically a triune, monotheistic God. For them, Caesar was God, the *epiphane*, the light, the august, the high and lifted potentate. Yet, how they dealt with the bodies of their citizens, at least before punishment for crime was meted out, was quite striking, especially with respect to how contrastably civil it was compared to America. For America, how it deals with the bodies of its marginalized (marginalized but not marginal) citizens reveals the truth of its theological paucity.

In addition to the Lucan account of the Acts of the Apostles, Matthew recounts in his Gospel how Jesus said, "Inasmuch as ye have done it unto one of the least of these my brethren, ye have done it unto me" (Matt 25:40 KJV). The problematics of the language of "least of" notwithstanding, Jesus's rhetoric stands to underscore how a nation can never be any greater than how it treats the bodies of those that do not possess privilege. It is in this way that America is theologically emaciated. And it is out of this experience that Du Bois felt immured in and by his Blackness. And it is out of this experience that my girlfriend and I, upon that fateful night, felt deracinated and dislocated (as seen in my essay "On a Summer Being Stolen"). It is out of this experience that Michael Brown was unjustly killed, his body wholly desecrated. It is the experience of a great many Black people who inhabit the United States.

To curtail these deleterious proclivities, perhaps America should transpose and develop Elisabeth Vasko's theorized methodology that she refers to as "active and attentive listening." She writes in her book *Beyond Apathy*:

---

68. Foucault, "Hermeneutic of the Subject," 100.

> The practice of deep listening is necessary for privileged elites in their efforts to become allies in the work of bringing about the kin-dom.[69]

Vasko uses this term "kin-dom" as opposed to kingdom because *kingdom* is immanently hierarchical and she seeks to adapt rather a relational model of anthropological relativism that foregoes kowtows and genuflections. She believes this is the redemptive work necessary to ameliorate the trenchant wounds of a barbarous past and hypocritical present that fester in the national household, where screams are colored in blood, staining the air across amber waves of grain. Therefore, if America is ever going to live into what it professes to be as a free, democratic society, Vasko maintains that he needs to adopt a model of radically progressive and liberative listening, a listening that is not self-serving or self-congratulating but that is real and complete and that considers those who understand the effects of sins it has committed—the oppressed, because the white person, the person of privilege, is "rendered incapable of making valid judgments on the character of sin [because for them] it is not a concrete reality." For Vasko, this listening can be the lighted avenue towards a redemptive theology for him, America, a theology for that "man in Appalachia, who feels that his whiteness has begun to lose its value,"[70] for that big city lawyer who feels that Spanish-speaking restaurant workers should go back to Mexico, for that woman in the Bay Area who feels it her duty to call the police for a barbecuing infraction or because a little girl did not procure a permit to sell lemonade, for that police officer who chauvinistically pressed his knee into the neck of a defenseless man for *eight minutes and forty-six seconds*—a theology that hears the lament of the oppressed, that they can't breathe, and by hearing finally institutes a reasoned and honest approach to granting observable citizenship to the Black person. However, this is at least a slightly naïve position to take, if only because if transposed to America, not as an aggregate of persons but as a distinct, singular personhood, it presumes that America possesses an anti-solipsistic, meritorious philosophy of life. It presumes that America would be invested enough or at all in its own betterment of self, in the Foucauldian sense, and not a manifest and documented hubristic being largely demonstrative of pernicious egoism and self-aggrandizement.

The English term *religion* derives from the Latin term *religare*, which, when translated literally, means "to bind again." Therefore, this state

---

69. Vasko, *Beyond Apathy*, 185.

70. Public theologian Ruby Sales uses this language to describe the phenomenon of whiteness as racial identity being in crisis in an interview with Krista Tippett entitled "Where Does It Hurt?"

adjudicated white supremacy is a tradition that actively seeks to enchain those who were once bound and binds even its participants in an inextricable moral quandary that has destroyed their collective capacity for truth and justice. Since this is an essay in response to America's innate endorsement of white supremacy as religion, I thought it would be apt to respond theologically to this white supremacist ecology of tradition and ritual with an ironic reading of the philosophy of a Nazi sympathizer, Martin Heidegger, a white supremacist in his own right:

> When tradition thus becomes master, it does so in such a way that what it "transmits" is made so inaccessible, proximally and for the most part, that it rather becomes concealed. Tradition takes what has come down to us and delivers it over to self-evidence; it blocks our access to those primordial "sources" from which the categories and concepts handed down to us have been in part quite genuinely drawn. Indeed it makes us forget that they have had such an origin, and makes us suppose that the necessity of going back to these sources is something which we need not even understand.[71]

It will be necessary, if the religion of white supremacy is to ever be meliorated, for the participants in the religion, namely the government, and the white person himself, particularly the 81 percent of white, male evangelicals who voted for Donald Trump (under whose leadership, white supremacists have emerged with greater rigor and force, culminating in the Unite the Right rally in Charlottesville, Virginia, resulting in the killing a protestor in August 2017), to evaluate the conspicuous ways in which it is confederate with white supremacy and how this tradition, exhibited as ritual, explained as religion, began its rampant and unremitting consequences. Thus, Heidegger unwittingly offers a solution to the unremitting legacy of racist liturgies, filled with tradition and ritual—destruction, and a very sensible and pragmatic destruction at that, "it's aim [...] positive [...] its negative function [remaining] unexpressed and indirect."[72] First, he posits that this brand of destruction as reformation of tradition must take place to provide lucidity of practice and to explain why what is practiced is practiced:

> If the question of Being is to have its own history made transparent, then this hardened tradition must be loosened up, and the concealments which it has brought about dissolved. We understand this task as one in which by taking the question of Being as our clue we are to destroy the traditional content of

71. Heidegger, *Being and Time*, 43.
72. Heidegger, *Being and Time*, 44.

ancient ontology until we arrive at those primordial experiences in which we achieved our first ways of determining the nature of Being—the ways which have guided us ever since.[73]

Here, simply put, Heidegger offers a path of redemption from tradition as master, and thus ritual and religion as master, by offering that there first must be the recognition and acknowledgement of what brought us to the state of staunch and mindless traditionalism, a remembrance of the factors that led to such observance.

In this regard, the white evangelical, which aids and abets the state as the only homogeneously religious group to endorse Trump for the presidency, may hold the key, in that they had the president's favor, to ending the sad liturgy that is costing American lives. It would be a theology rooted in the prophecy of Haggai, compelling men to "Consider [their] ways . . . build the house."[74] Perhaps it is possible for America to build a new house, a place of worship where all peoples can come and fellowship, that is not built on supremacy but on justice and peace.

Too drastic? If the invocation of a noted Nazi sympathizer's philosophical commitments is offensive and jarring, perhaps that quality redounds to just how ridiculous all this is: that white supremacy exists at all, that white supremacy could be described as a religion, that Black people are often tasked with bearing the brunt of white people's willful ineptitude on the matter of race when they themselves had nothing to do with its creation, that we are still being gunned down in the street by the state, that we feel compelled to attempt to convince anyone of our infallible humanity—it is offensive, is it not? However, let us not look to the hills for an answer but let us look to ourselves. If you are white and reading this and you do not like the Heideggerian conclusion, think back to Foucault and Bourdieu: examine yourself and witness how your daily practices make you a faith-filled participant in the religion of white supremacy, how your very actions are believing in earnest for you, how the lack of foam around your lips and Nazi paraphernalia in your garage makes you no less of an adherent to the religion of white supremacy, no less complicit in all the social ills it discloses. I invite you now to practice a new way, a way that will fully enfranchise and uplift the rights and privileges of Black people across this country economically, politically, and socially. Even if you feel that you cannot believe in such a way at this precise moment, if it feels too difficult to relinquish any of your position of privilege, I urge you just to try it, and allow the practice to believe for you and sanctify you and save you.

73. Heidegger, *Being and Time*, 44.
74. Hag 1:8 NRSV.

At the outset, one critique of some of the authors I have mentioned here is that, while they attempt to explain with ardor certain injustices of inequity that plague the land, they do not effectively speak to the Black experience. So, while Nussbaum is naming, Laborde is thematizing, and Vasko is prescribing, none of these scholars seem to confront with vigor the challenges that the American racial bias as violence against Black people has caused.

Rather, there seems to be a denial, at the very least, on the part of Vasko, which does not allow there to be a liberative chorus with the other two scholars. Again, the denial of culpability is the denial of anthropology (for the Black person in America) and elicits no real incentive for change. Further, it removes the executor of the act of violence, racism, and bigotry so far from responsibility, from the act itself, that the executor, in this case the religious adherent, can never and will never come to terms with what his worshipful service has wrought. Therefore, he will continue to commit these acts with no knowledge or appreciation of their inherent invidious and insidious nature. Here, there is a sin of omission, and there is a sin of commission, both ensconced in denial. So that when Michael Brown was shot and killed, for example, I posit that there is no other way that that could have gone. Thus, what this essay attempts to wrangle is acknowledgement. What is there that still pervades the philosophical moorings of America that allows these things that cannot be to exist? When Michael Brown was killed, that happened in no other way than it could, not because of ontological Blackness, but because of ontological whiteness. This ontological whiteness exudes itself in a manner that clings to privilege, that exudes disgust and fear that is ultimately deliberate, because white privilege is concomitant with white supremacy that is in fact a religion. So, in its own way, America is a constitutional theocracy, "where a religion is formally enshrined in the state," and not a democratic republic. There is an ecology of whiteness as supremacy that needs to be addressed, and once this work is begun it will culminate in a liberative political theology for Black people and a redemptive theology for white people and the nation with simultaneity. If this ecology of whiteness as supremacy is not addressed, challenged, and changed, if white people do not give up their whiteness, which is tied to supremacy and domination, then the consequences will no doubt be like the words brought back into popular consciousness uttered by one of my ancestors long ago: "God gave Noah the rainbow sign. No more water, fire next time."

Addendum (January 6, 2021)

A Tale as Old as Whiteness Itself

In my introduction I made the following note:

> In *Interpretation Theory*, Paul Ricœur theorizes that written language serves a different role than the locutionary, illocutionary, and perlocutionary functions of spoken language. He compares the written word to the Renaissance paintings of Jesus, Mary the mother of Jesus, the Apostle Paul, the Apostle John, and others. Those iconographies, he suggests, were not those people but a mythologized interpretation of those people, through that narrativization lifted to another register of meaning and significance. The painters, be they Da Vinci or Raphael, were looking back at Jesus and Paul through their mind's eye and offering their explanation of who those beings were to them, lifting them to a place of empyrean mythos. This for Ricœur is the functionality of the written word. If we look at monuments as the written word, according to Ricœur, as texts themselves, we can be reminded that the monuments of Confederate soldiers are not the soldiers; they are merely interpretations of the men they represent, lifted to a place of myth. Therefore, Confederate monuments came years later after the Civil War. Their artisans, looking to mythologize and valorize those people, adhering more to memory and interpretation (through a racist hermeneutic) than to factual history, sought to make their own iconography.

This is why Trump (and Trumpism) leaving office will not deflate his significance in the hearts of followers.

His being voted out actually strengthens his image and pre-fascist meditations.

Without him being available with such high visibility in the seat of American power, his followers are now able to make an iconography of him, transmuting him symbolically into a deified martyr, an empyrean myth, able to receive any and all of the significations they wish to impute to him.

He becomes whatever they need him to be—

King Arthur.

Robin Hood.

Jesse James.

Jesus of Nazareth.

Thus, in this way, Trump will be more valuable to his followers, increasingly radicalized by the religion of white supremacy, out of office than when he was as president.

I mean.

Did you see it?

Did you see it when they stormed one of the most vaunted monuments of American democracy?

They even brought a cross and gallows (complete with a hangman's noose) to the Capitol.

What a strange dialectic. And yet, not so strange.

It's the embodiment and fulfillment of a quote from Kelly Brown Douglas in her book *What's Faith Got to Do with It?: Black Bodies/Christian Souls*:

"Christianity's classical atonement tradition [mitigated that] . . . a crowd that lynches . . . would not immediately repulse . . . God. A God that sanctions a human sacrifice as brutal as crucifixion can serve as a divine ally for those who make such a sacrifice—even a sacrifice as horrific as lynching."

A cross and gallows.

They look at the Bible not as a living document in constant search of locating freedom and justice but as a lifeless tome that supports and emboldens the narrative of exceptionalism and unimpeachable, inherent righteousness of Christians for Christianity's sake.

What farce. What madness.

What a perfect religion for white supremacy.

That Jesus somehow empowers some to take life, and by proxy, take anything that they want because they believe they have some primacy of moral rightness just because they are Christian, that they can dispense justice and hold the keys to mercy with simultaneity, is the worst sort of narcissism.

This dark, twisted fantasy, this deleterious delusion that bids them lynch and pray, terrorize and talk God, is galling.

It is a tale as old as whiteness itself.

I am still shocked, but I am not surprised.

Whiteness is a child's game that claims victory when it has rigged the system of play. Or perhaps it is the child himself, petulant, querulous, repeatedly punching and insulting his classmates, brought to a place of shock and horror when they respond in kind.

Whiteness needs to be abolished.

Now some smart person is going to come along and suggest that if whiteness needs to be abolished that Blackness needs to be abolished as well.

To that I respond that whiteness was manufactured specifically by a few people for a few people to get money and power. That's it.

Blackness has been refined through generations to give people hope to face the day and to teach people to always seek justice and to resist oppression.

Whiteness was invented.

Blackness was cultivated.

What is not destructive but instructive should never be abolished.

Whiteness needs to be abolished.

And when it finally is those who held whiteness as their own for so long will marvel at the fact that they're still alive without it.

6.

To My Sweet Boy

(I know you'll never read this.)

We are each other's harvest: we are each other's business: we are each other's magnitude and bond.

—Gwendolyn Brooks, "Paul Robeson"

I remember you as you were, both short and tall, legs and arms anime long, an angular, joyous parade of geometry wafting through fluorescent lighting. My sweet boy. You daydreamed too often, completed classwork too seldom, sitting only two chairs in front of my desk, thickly bespectacled, expertly aloof. Do you remember how you would pick your nose and taste the fruits of your labor, smack dab in the middle of class, your attention from this realism so far removed, your mind in such a distant but familiar world, that when your classmates would whisper revile against you for the nasty habit, I would prevent them from making you a martyr of social taboos? When I called you once to my desk after class, to bring this penchant for putrid picking to your attention, informing you that this indeed was not the behavior becoming of a 9th grader, no matter how embarrassed your petrified person appeared to be, no matter how speechless, no matter how many times I had to reprimand you for succeeding at failing to ever be on task, you would always say when class ended, more than most others of my students, "Have a good day, Mr. Baugh," or "Great class, Mr. Baugh." My sweet boy. I remember you as you were. Perhaps that memory of you is nothing more than me looking through a glass darkly. Perhaps that is the problem.

>06/15/2018
>
>My Dear Friends,
>
>As you know, I am very fond of words—their shape, their form, their many armies of significations are my morning's salutation and my evening's rest. Yet, for the life of me I cannot seem to put to paper all that this, my departing, has evoked. I spent last night searching for the words to carry my gratitude to you, words that would in no unclear terms explain what I feel in this moment, which can only be characterized as thankfulness.
>
>So, let me say it this way, simply—thank you. Thank you for listening, for hearing, for being there at the ready to be taught, day in and day out. Thank you for wrestling with concepts that seemed to have nothing to do with English, for allowing yourself to be challenged, for allowing yourselves to grow. What warriors you are, what *scholars*. Your labor has not gone unnoticed.
>
>For what we accomplished together in *our* classroom, a space I hope was a place of liberation for your hearts and minds, where you could not only learn subject matter but also how inestimably valuable you are in a world that so often seeks to suggest otherwise—thank you. For the smiles you gave—thank you. (They frequently rescued my day.) For all of the times you just wanted to sit and talk—thank you. For all the times you just wanted to be around me when I did not want to be around myself—thank you. For all the laughs—thank you. For your youthful energy—thank you. For your unconquerable spirit—thank you.
>
>There are so many things left unsaid, so many more journeys we could have taken together. Seasons change, my students. The summer approaches and I must go; your summer has only begun. What adventures await you in this life are limitless, what potential you have to achieve your dreams, endless.
>
>Your dreams (this is my final lesson for you), your dreams—never let them die. Never neglect them. Never listen to they that would suggest your dreams are too big, too vast to be achieved. What do they know? We know that *all* things are possible to them that believe. Therefore, be bold and give no thought to giving up, ever.
>
>Cling to that which is good; hate that which is evil. Stand up for the weak. Have no patience for bullies, for those who would seek to oppress others because they consider themselves

powerful. Know your worth and no one will ever be able to buy you. Be humble and be grateful, for these are the avenues to blessing. Love. Forgive, even yourself—we're all still figuring this thing out. Honor your parents. Be kind. Forget to be afraid. Remember that you have a voice.

Do good in this world, my dearest ones, my only ones, my Beloved. I shall never forget any of you. I carry each of you with me always.

Love,

Mr. Baugh

This is the note I left all my students, as you know (being one of them), upon my departure from teaching at Nansemond River High School to pursue a second master's degree at Boston University. In the interregnum since my departing, I have periodically used the same mobile application I used to send this letter, called Remind 101, communicating with my former students, whom I have taught through the years, to encourage them in the process of their schooling, sending congratulations letters to those who graduate, offering tutoring services to those who need extra help when the state test approaches. This you also know.

Flashforward to the long, protracted year of 2020, a century's worth of tribulations condensed into a hockey season. I sent out a message on the app about literacy and how crucially important it is to read books to learn and as the only avenue to becoming significantly contributing and engaged members of society, to become agents of change, particularly in the pressing matters of this time: persistent racial inequalities, systemic police brutality against people of color, and generational poverty. Consequently, my message contained a reading list, a database of free books all written by Black authors that I had discovered online. Students I had taught from years ago expressed their interest and thanks for my engaging their literacy with a curated compendium of books about philosophy, economics, politics, consciousness, sociology, abolition, America, liberation, and your response was unlike all the rest—your response was to *instantly* deride it. When I saw that you had messaged me, my heart was overjoyed because I had not heard from you in two years. My sweet boy. I thought you would have expressed enthusiasm about the reading list. Instead, you berated me and scoffed at the very notion of the importance Black authorship, responding:

> Me (Mr.) Baugh, I would strongly encourage kids to read a variety of things not just those listed in your previous message. The sooner that everyone realizes that ALL Lives matter and that tearing down a statue will not change the past or the future the

better off our society will be. One life is not worth more than another regardless of the color of someone's skin . . . . I believe the sooner that people stop talking about black lives, blue lives and such the better off we will be. There haven't been slaves in my lifetime, my mothers, my grandmothers or great grandmothers. Removing statues does not change what has happened. It is simply people destroying property that is not their property.

My sweet boy. Your words cut like the apogee of your elbows through air whenever you would waltz across the linoleum, brandless shoes untied, backpack like Atlas donning the planet. The nonsense about racist statues being removed from the public sphere being unnecessary notwithstanding, what is so striking in this message is that never did I suggest that my students should never read any authors other than these Black authors; I simply suggested that the books on the reading list, books written by Toni Morrison, James Baldwin, Cornel West, Frantz Fanon, Angela Davis, Octavia Butler, and many others, would be most advantageous to read, emphasizing the criticality of literacy and sensitivity to being dialogical with authors who may not look like you as indispensable to being an effective member of any civilized society. Yet, your interpretation of my well-intentioned message was, ironically, that it prioritized certain voices over others, when there is no way a thinking person, one not adhering to an ecology of self-importance, would ever come to that conclusion. Case and point—you issued your statement that "ALL LIVES MATTER" when I never suggested anything otherwise. Your invective, colored with the pretext of civil concern, suggesting that all lives matter emerged from me simply issuing a reading list full of Black authors. Think about that. Why would the presence of Black authorship warrant that response, if it is true that *all* lives matter? Quite strange, indeed. My sweet boy.

So, I began to think about how young you still are, and how you are moving into your senior year now, and that this system of fallacious reasoning has already substantiated your personal hermeneutic of suspicion of literacy, of ethnicity, of culture, of scholarship, of identity, of personhood, of society—and even of justice—how you are not reading books now, how you may never begin to read books, you so stringently dismissing the very idea of reading even one book from the list. I began thinking about selfhood, specifically the selfhood that whiteness imparts, whiteness as an ecology of being, whiteness as a metaphor for power, whiteness as property, and I began to wonder if there are any other parallels to it in nature, if it is comparable to the selfhood feature of instinctiveness seen elsewhere in the animal kingdom:

Tigers are said to be dangerous at six months, lethal just a year later. Spitting cobra are known to viscerally spew an extremely toxic venom into the eyes of humans upon hatching. How early does whiteness begin to seek Blackness as its prey; at what age does it begin its lifelong quest to silence the Black voice? Why is it so easy for even ostensibly well-meaning white people to live into a space where they totally reject notions of Black humanity and see any exhibition of self-possession and self-preservation among Black people, even Black literature, as threatening? I do not have the perfect answers to these questions.

I do know that not talking about the matter of race in American life will not make the concept of race dissolve nor the persistent challenges of racism in American society disappear (the very reason there have not been any enslaved Africans in America in your lifetime, or your grandmother's lifetime, or even your great-grandmother's lifetime, is that people, principally Black people, confronted that unspeakable system of oppression, which hastened its end). That is a fantast's delusion, a false narrative created in the minds of a group of immature adherents to the myth of American exceptionalism—that somehow to have faults as a nation, which must be confronted and rectified, lowers the selfhood of the citizen, lowers the nation. This brand of thinking is both inaneness and violence.

It is, finally, at long last, time for America to grow up. But first, my sweet boy, you will have to.

7.

A Theology of Rejoicing

For ourselves and for humanity, comrades, we must make a new start, develop a new way of thinking, and endeavor to create a new man.

—FRANTZ FANON, THE WRETCHED OF THE EARTH

To break the back of such a dire, hegemonic code that has integrated itself so pervasively into the American societal psyche, to theologically confront with aplomb the religion of white supremacy in America, calls for a hermeneutic(method of interpretation) of *violence*. Though, violence has lost its bite. We are flooded with its wildcat imagery in all segments of society at large: in the arts, in news coverage, in our morning commute, in boasts of coolly rendered micro-aggressions. It is ubiquitous, violence. Yet, though we may have become desensitized to its harrowing and unsettling touch, it is no less gruesome than it has always been. No less austere or severe or ravaging. No less *necessary*. What I am proposing is a theology of preaching that can be extended beyond the pulpit, that is animated by a hermeneutic that must be a violent occasion. As it is written, "The kingdom suffers violence, and the violent take it by force." Therefore, the homiletical response as theological retort to such a miserable social condition as white supremacy as religion must be animated and informed by a hermeneutic that is violent. I want this hermeneutic to be a violent affair. I know what I am saying—it should serve to unhouse, dislocate, and decenter, and shatter the hegemonic superstructures of text and textual interpretation and influence the dominant culture. This constructive violence is much like the violence that Frantz Fanon describes in his book *The Wretched of the Earth*:

"At the individual level, violence is a cleansing force. It rids the colonized of their inferiority complex, of their passive and despairing attitude. It emboldens them, and restores their self-confidence. Even if the armed struggle has been symbolic, and even if they have been demobilized by rapid decolonization, the people have time to realize that liberation was the achievement of each and every one and no special merit should go to the leader. Violence hoists the people up to the level of leader. Hence their aggressive tendency to distrust the system of protocol that young governments are quick to establish. When they have used violence to achieve national liberation, the masses allow nobody to come forward as "liberator."[1]

The liberator is in the interpreter and the interpreter is in the liberator. It is a highly democratic process. And violence is a constitutive element in the pursuit of liberation, a violence that is constitutive to the ends of fortifying a way of looking at text that revolutionizes how text is appropriated and orientated to the pulling down the strongholds of textual constraints, which serve to empower some at the expense of emaciating many.

The violence of this hermeneutic that is necessary to rescripting the dominant reality may lead to what must be developed into a lexicon that has been given time to ferment in the hearts and minds of the citizenry—a lexicon indexical of a language that is only redemptive, that is only liberative, that is only constructive and generative. It must be through a concerted use of language that allows those who are undervoiced to be benefited. This was August Wilson's thinking when he introduced the character of King Hedley in his now canonical tragedy *Seven Guitars*.

King Hedley, a supporting character in the play, is a Black man living as a failed musician in the forties and friendly with some successful musicians. He has a monologue about why his father named him King. It is so that white people who routinely call grown men *boys* during this time would have to refer to him as royalty, even if they did not want to. Because of the Saussurean langue, the codified requirements of language—they would have to call him *king*.

As we upend the cultural hegemony that is language that disparages others in our communities, we must fashion the language in such a way that it innately, inherently, and intrinsically benefits those who are on the margins of society. The ramification of this hermeneutic posture should yield results as such that one has no other option than to live into a theological space conducive to anti-hegemony and practiced, lived justice. In

---

1. Fanon, *Wretched of the Earth*, 119.

this linguistic theological and philosophical space, I have to call you king. I have to call you queen. This explodes the normative thinking that has been dogmatically patriarchal and favoring the powerful—male, straight, white, land-owning, wealthy, etcetera, etcetera, etcetera. Conversely, choosing not to call one queen or king (so to speak) reveals an arrogance that is intransigent, adamantine, and grossly inflexible and shows forth one's unwillingness to truly be about the liberation of the oppressed, in substance, upholding rather than upending the power structures of their present ecclesiology and of society at large, which is a white power structure, thus shoring up, in essence, the religion of white supremacy in this nation.

However, it does not always work out the intended way. Wilson reveals how anyone can become a tool of insidious white patriarchal normatives, that seek to dominate and desecrate others, a phenomenon King Hedley explains he incurred in his own life:

> HEDLEY: I killed a man once. A black man. I am not sorry I killed him.
> RUBY: What you kill him for? Elmore killed Leroy for nothing.
> HEDLEY: He would not call me King. He laughed to think a black man could be King. I did not want to lose my name, so I told him to call me the name my father gave me, and he laugh. He would not call me King, and I beat him hard with a stick. That is what cost me my time with a woman. After that I don't tell nobody my name is King. It is a bad thing. Everybody say Hedley crazy cause he black. Because he know the place of the black man is not at the foot of the white man's boot. Maybe it is not all right in my head sometimes. Because I don't like the world. I don't like what I see from the people. The people is too small. I always want to be a big man. Like Jesus Christ was a big man. He was the son of the Father. I too. I am the son of my father. Maybe Hedley never going to be big like that. But for himself inside. That place where you live your own special life. I would be happy to be big there. And maybe my child, if it be a boy, he would be big like Moses. I think about that. Somebody have to be the father of the man to lead the black man out of bondage. Marcus Garvey have a father. Maybe if I could not be like Marcus Garvey then I could be the father of someone who would not bow down to the white man. Maybe I could be the father of the messiah.[2]

What's in a name? People live and die according to names. What we choose to name people, what we choose to name things, is very important. We must

---

2. Wilson, *Seven Guitars*, 2.1.

cultivate a language that normalizes a liberation ethic, that does not further establish hierarchies but that ennobles individuals within our communities.

VISITING A FORMER SEMINARY PROFESSOR

I had the opportunity recently to audit Professor James Henry Harris's homiletics class at the Samuel DeWitt Proctor School of Theology at Virginia Union University. Dr. Harris, whose own work focuses on interpreting texts, had the students read Song of Solomon chapter 1, verses 1–4, and provide their interpretation of the text orally:

> The song of songs, which is Solomon's. Let him kiss me with the kisses of his mouth: for thy love is better than wine. Because of the savour of thy good ointments thy name is as ointment poured forth, therefore do the virgins love thee. Draw me, we will run after thee: the king hath brought me into his chambers: we will be glad and rejoice in thee, we will remember thy love more than wine: the upright love thee.[3]

Almost as a rule, the students' interpretation of this text was one that was not imaginative, was not inventive, or expressive of any ally-ship with those who live at the margins of society. Rather, it evidenced a deep and abiding commitment to the reinforcement of certain cultural normatives that promoted the tyranny of the male gaze, patriarchy, and paternalism, rejecting pluralism at all costs. When I interjected, suggesting that the woman is being used here as a tool to demonstrate male dominance and power, that her very being had been reduced to a fetishizing affection of maleness, that she has been stripped of all personality and objectified to the point of automated, soulless worship of masculinity, and that a hermeneutic that suggests otherwise is specious and suspicious, I was excoriated by the students. What was most striking to me, paradoxically, the loudest and militating voices against me were women. Now, I freely appreciate these women and their free moral agency and autonomy. It just seemed to me in that moment that, through their interpretation of that text, they had become confederate with the same power structure they seek to overcome, even a power structure that both bullies and belies them daily, which I found perplexing. They did not look for the liberative opportunity in the text, for a hermeneutic that could be enlivening and enriching for those marginalized in society at large, of which demographic they are a part; they simply regurgitated Mad Gab talking points of hegemonic theologies which had been passed down

---

3. Song 1:1–4 KJV.

to them down through the patriarchal generations, so that even to their own demise as free, autonomous, moral agents, they choose to uphold systems of textuality that are destructive. But I learned long ago to stay out of women's business. So, I digress.

Bad theology is the theology of empire. It is a theology that favors the strong over the weak. (Even in a simple class-based exercise like that.) It is a theology that knows only how to win and believes that nothing can be learned from losing. Simply put, if you are not an ally to those that are oppressed, then your theology is bad, because it favors the powerful over the weak when God resists the proud.

Therefore, we should apply a communist, proletarian hermeneutic to our preaching. One that resists the proud, one that resists all hegemony of interpretation informed by the bourgeoisie's and the petty bourgeoisie's ambition that is simply reductionist and ultimately steeped in the past, subjugating some, exalting some others. One that does not holt to a selfish, "get mine" sensibility, largely reflective of free-market capitalist subjectivation. A communist hermeneutic is what it should be like, a hermeneutic for the working class. A hermeneutic that looks to the future. A hermeneutic that does not look to maintain strongholds of the past established by the dominant class and their interests. Though I am not a communist, what I like about Marx's analysis of capitalism is how he shows that it creates and deepens class distinctions that at one point in time had not been there and that these distinctions are ultimately destructive to the freedom of humankind. Consequently, many preachers are preaching with a particularly capitalistic hermeneutic in more ways than one, shoring up the interests of the bourgeoisie, sometimes without even knowing it. This when most people in American life are at some level working-class people, pitted against each other and commoditized by the holders of the capital, selling themselves as merchandise of service. No different than any other commodity. We are in this way counted as sheep for the slaughter, "slaves of the bourgeois class, and of the bourgeois state . . . daily and hourly enslaved by the foreman, and above all, by the individual bourgeois manufacturer himself."[45] This is why

4. Marx and Engels, *Communist Manifesto*, 70.

5. I know this statement is very controversial. The very word *communism* has become a symbol that has a great many negative significations imparted into it through the years. It is impossible to even mention communism or anything that sounds remotely close to it (i.e., Bernie Sanders's democratic socialism and his second failed presidential bid) without folk instinctively riling up with anger, calling you everything but a child of God, deeming you unpatriotic and amoral, while foaming at the mouth. But just because I favor the prescient and insightful analysis of capitalism from a philosopher and poet from the past does not make me a communist. I am not a communist. However, I think that Marx's thought is indispensable if we are to understand the ravenous

our preaching must be one of liberation, our cultivated witness, prophetic. Our worth does not derive from wealth, that is, material wealth. It never has. It never will, particularly Black people, when capitalism was never meant to benefit us at all.[6] Thus, it becomes clear that the job of the preacher must be to preach from a perspective informed by a hermeneutic that reminds the people that they are more than just a number itemized on a spreadsheet of some petty bourgeoisie underboss on a meaningless job somewhere. That we should not distanciate ourselves from the individual aims of one another as members all of the working class. We cannot further create class distinction in and out of the church and reinforce hierarchies where there should be none, for to do so would be representative of bad theology. In short, if your theology is not attempting to liberate or beatify anyone, if it is the pabulum of church theology or the confederate meaninglessness of state theology, it is worthless. How do you know if your theology is good theology?—If it seeks to liberate and be a prophetic witness for justice and mercy in the world. What is more, in addition to being simply bad theology, the prevailing theological position in that class that evening disadvantages the especial and essential perspective from the margins that should be gleaned by the society at large.[7] This is the very kind of marginality that can be used to the advantage of the oppressed. It is the same brand of marginality that Katie Geneva Cannon expresses in her great text *Katie's Canon*, a collection of essays with a synthetic thesis, in which she explores how there is a natural transformative theology that does accompany Black womanhood that could be beneficial to all people. It is a theology not encumbered by the presuppositions of predominance and preeminence as found in the moorings of imperialism and capitalism; it is a theology rooted in the reality of suffering and otherness, that has had time to be among the "least of these," that has germinated and grown to a mature fulness. Other theologies, which often

---

beast that is capitalism and its many permutations, which include how we interpret and respond to the different parts of the society in which we live.

6. In "Racism and Economics," an essay in *Katie's Canon*, Cannon dialogues with the thought of sociologist Oliver Cox and explores the ways in which racism and greed worked together to create the idea of race, which led to American chattel slavery, a white supremacist institution, which is what led to capitalism, becoming its engine. So, in that way, racism predicated capitalism. She further explores the ways in which capitalism as an economic system has historically *never* benefited people of color across the globe, particularly Black peoples of color. Thus, Cannon offers an open invitation for us to imagine a more excellent economic system and a more excellent way of advantaging voices, perspectives, and peoples.

7. I am also indebted to the thought of Lety Russell, who explores this idea of redemptive marginality in her wonderful book *Church in the Round: Feminist Interpretation of the Church*.

are exclusive and uninformed by the light of any real adversity, thus claustral and untried, close in on themselves. Womanist theology is a philosophical boon for the human populace, "a process by which [the interlocutor brings] this kind of knowing about African American women into relation with justice-praxis for members of our species and the wider environment in which we are situated in order to resist conditions that thwart life."[8] A theology that is not mode of resistance is one that is silly, saccharine, senile, and toothless. In the book, Cannon offers a rousing glimpse in this regard as to how a theology is not simply conceived, it must be developed through the rigors and trials of a life that is not trivial. It must be forged in the cauldron of life in the face of death, a theology sensitized to the unreality of superiority. It may look like the womanist theology of Katie Cannon. It may look like Hecuba, repurposing the cultural hegemony of her day, which was not textless, repurposing her marginality as a woman in a male-dominated patriarchal and misogynistic society.

HECUBA, WOMANHOOD, AND THE IRONIC PRICE OF THE PATRIARCHY

In *Hecuba* by Euripides we see that woman has been distinctly relegated to that of contrariety. She has been defined by the terms of men, even in death. Through the words of Talthybius the messenger we read that when Polyxena, the daughter of Hecuba, is executed, she "took good heed to fall with maiden grace, hiding from gaze of man what modest maiden must." Yet in the throes of emerging decedent, the woman must conform the very spatial morphological expression to appease the fragility of a man's domineering expectations of her. We witness that not only is a woman not her own in life, but also that in death she must live up to a man's standard, as her unconscious sarcophagus of flesh stumbles to the floor. This reveals that a woman's body is known to be a man's, he categorically objectifying her—if she is dead, her spirit, her mind has absconded her body, and thus she is no longer present-at-hand, she can no further be responsible for her actions in a lifeless state. This seems a hackneyed and listless thought until one considers the severe implications that are condign to this line of reasoning: if a woman is to deport herself according to man's standard, even as she is dead, it reveals that the man, concerned with her body, and only concerned with her body (as the spirited, appetitive regions of her being are no more extant within her physicality) is limited in this view of her. This may explain why men of that time and in modernity are so greatly possessive of

---

8. Cannon, *Katie's Canon*, 141.

women—they only see them as possessions, which, as Aristotle explains, is one of the categories or predicaments, thus immediately putting to mind an acerbic, troubled, and truculent relationship with said possession that could be no other way. Therefore, the man creates the atmosphere into which he abuses, discounts, and otherwise negates what he claims he cares for, for no other reason than his woefully limited scope of what that possession is, not a woman but a *thing*.

In *The Second Sex*, existentialist philosopher Simone de Beauvoir suggests that a woman's facticity, the essence of who she is, has been dictated to her by a man, therefore causing her to become "other." She is not a man, and her femininity is not her own for it has been designated her by a man. Through the dialectical process of self-construction, woman realizes that man is never defined in the light of femininity but that woman is invariably defined in terms of masculine desires—the way she dresses, the way she walks, the way she talks, the way she wears her makeup, all are ways that are reflective of the woman discovering that she is to live up to man's standard and that, if she deviates from that standard, it can be dangerous for her. Nevertheless, Beauvoir maintains that because of these strictures placed upon women in a paternalistic, phallocentric, patriarchal society, it is not enough to be born a woman, but one must become a woman through the actions she takes to exert, exude, and exhibit her immanent and inherent freedom.

Consequently, when we observe Hecuba in the final scene of the play, hastening the denouement, creating the opportunity to reclaim womanhood, defining how she the woman desires it to be, we see her not only bringing justice to her son's (Polydorus) murderer in a purely rectificatory way, but also forging a new identity for womanhood that is closer to its actuality abstract from its patriarchal facticity. She embodies the notion that woman is man's servant, that "men have always held all the concrete powers; from patriarchy's earliest times they have deemed it useful to keep woman in a state of dependence [with] their codes . . . set up against her,"[9] and uses this structural and political restriction in an ironic way to mobilize the other women loyal to her to exact her revenge, demonstrating that man's preeminence becomes his own downfall, his dominance is his own undoing. I want this hermeneutic to be a violence against the oppressor, using the oppressor's position of perceived dominance against him, and, like Hecuba, pluck out the oppressor's eyes. It is only then that new eyes can be imparted through which to view the world with eyes unclouded by prejudice and bigotry. What was meant for evil can be repurposed and reoriented for good.

---

9. Beauvoir, *Second Sex*, 159.

BLACK SACRED RHETORIC AND A THEOLOGY OF REJOICING

Nevertheless, finally, once an appropriate hermeneutic has been established, it is through the lens of Black sacred rhetoric that we finally construct a theology that can offer redemption for marginalized and desperate communities. It was Paul Tillich in his *The Courage to Be* that posited the only way that we are able to experience society is through our community. However, if one's community is maligned and marginalized and disparaged, how effective could the oculus of community, a scope through which to view and experience the world, ever possibly be? For example, when Michael Brown was killed by Darren Wilson, that was injustice enough; the greater injustice, however, was leaving his bloody, gored, lifeless body out in the street for over four hours, on the very street where he had walked countless times before with friends, in a neighborhood where he had his being, devastating a community that had watched him grow only to become a phantom before their eyes, lost forever to the tide of white supremacy, animated as fear, justified as lawful activity. (How could the members of that community ever drive down Canfield Drive again and not see the haunting image of Michael Brown's bullet-addled remains lying there desecrated before them?) Thus, it becomes strikingly clear that there must be some galvanizing offering to uplift disparaged communities, particularly communities of color, specifically Black communities. The hermeneutic now explained affords us the ability to explore how it can be preached through a homiletical theology.

Black sacred rhetoric, or the art of African American preaching, is filled with ingenious innovations. Most relevant for this theology, however, is what lies at the conclusion of its sermonic discourse. However, it is not in the perlocutionary inventiveness of the "whoop," that melodic and mellifluous, highly rhythmic and metered intoning of gutturals and soaring sonorous polyphony that proceeds from the pulpit, ending the sermon. Rather, it, the genius, is found in the illocutionary substance of the celebration act that bookends most sermons that practice a homiletical methodology consistent with Black sacred rhetoric. Indeed, there are lessons to be learned from this ingenious rhetorical, philosophical, and theological commitment found in Black sacred rhetoric that can be transposed to meet the existential plight of disparaged communities, and that is this: whatever in the life of the community that is commensurate with death, destruction, or despair is irrelevant because *no matter how something is begun, it can and will always end in the victory that is celebration*:

> The African American preaching tradition of celebrative design has untold riches and experience in celebrative emotional process, affirmative images, and the practice of celebration.[10]

However, the import of this methodology moves beyond preaching, and it becomes a theology of rejoicing. It is not only a way of preaching but of living, of providing a prophetic witness for disparaged communities in every realm of society that weaponizes celebration to confront that which affronts epistemologically, politically, culturally, and economically the verdant existential experience of Black communities across the United States.

This theology is inspired by the homiletical methodological commitments of Black sacred rhetoric, principally as disclosed by Frank A. Thomas in his book *They Like to Never Quit Praisin' God: The Role of Celebration in Preaching*. In it, Thomas explores the ways in which celebration "is the culmination of the sermonic design, where a moment is created in which the remembrance of a redemptive past and/or the conviction of a liberated future transforms the events immediately experienced. The sermonic design is an emotional process that culminates in a moment of celebration when the good news (the *assurance* of grace) intensifies in core belief until one has received an inner assurance, affirmation, courage, and a feeling of empowerment." He looks at how celebration, as a part of the preached moment is highly constructive, that it engenders "a feeling of empowerment," instills "assurance," and that through celebration one "experiences oneself as victorious (that is, saved, set free, healed, encouraged, and so on) regardless of the external tragic circumstances of life."[11] Exposing how celebration in the preached moment is uplifting and upbuilding and fundamentally constructive by design, Thomas maintains that celebration is "the joyful and ecstatic reinforcement of the truth already taught and delivered in the main body of the sermon."[12] Providing an example from the prescient and powerful "Mountaintop" sermon delivered by Martin Luther King Jr. in Memphis the night before he was to be assassinated, Thomas demonstrates how the dynamics of celebration have their operable forms in an elucidation of the peroration of the King speech, which famously ends with the line "Mine eyes have seen the glory of the coming of the Lord":

> After experiencing the liberating power of this celebrative moment, the people marched, convinced that the power of God experienced in core belief was more powerful than the evil in the world. Celebration *transformed* their present reality, allowing

---

10. Thomas, *They Like to Never Quit*, 54.
11. Thomas, *They Like to Never Quit*, 49.
12. Thomas, *They Like to Never Quit*, 108.

them to face evil with courage and boldness. In the meeting, there was information and strategizing, to be sure, but the spirit of the meeting was that of celebration and victory. It was this celebrative spirit that they carried during the march, primarily voiced through singing and praying, that helped them to creatively confront and overcome evil.[13]

This is the constructive capacity of celebration as rejoicing—the culmination of a methodological approach to preaching that edifies, reformats, and restores. The method that leads to sermon celebration that Frank Thomas employs could aptly be called Situation-Complication-Resolution-Celebration, or SCRC. The SCRC method of sermon preparation explained by Thomas is as follows:

For centuries upon centuries and generations upon generations, human beings have noticed a pattern in life: one experiences a situation, there occurs some complication of that situation, and then invariably there is some kind of resolution of the complication. This pattern is so pervasive in the human experience that it has become embedded in the intuitive aspect of human awareness as an instinct or a form. I believe the form to be intuitive because it is found in human civilization worldwide, from the earliest creation myths of the ancient world, to the plays of Sophocles, to the parables of Jesus, to the tragedies of Shakespeare, . . . to modern television sitcoms, to multimillion-dollar movie productions, to the sound bytes of politics and political campaigns. One of the most powerful constructs in human communication is the intuitive form of situation-complication-resolution.[14]

According to Thomas, the situation is quite foundational. It is the substratum, the inexorable and inimitable event that secures the subject matter of the sermon. It is here that the exposition of the narrativity of the message is plotted and the trajectory established. However, it is not until the next movement of motility in the narrative form of the sermonic discourse, the complication, that the tension and central conflict of the sermon is discovered "and suspense is added to the drama."[15] This, in Thomas's view, is of supreme importance in the sermon, as it builds suspense in the sermon, and suspense is vital to adhering to the precepts of Black sacred rhetoric, that is, that it must be an *experiential* affair. In African American preaching,

13. Thomas, *They Like to Never Quit*, 51.
14. Thomas, *They Like to Never Quit*, 72.
15. Thomas, *They Like to Never Quit*, 73.

> The Bible comes alive by means of an eyewitness style of picture painting and narration. The preacher stirs the five senses, and, as a result, the hearer does not just hear about John the Baptist in the past biblical times; rather, John the Baptist is present in the room, seen, heard, touched, and felt by all. I heard James Forbes Jr. tell the story that Gardner Taylor was preaching the biblical story of the prodigal son. In a particularly poignant moment, Forbes recounts that Dr. Taylor said, "Look, the boy is coming up the road now!" Forbes says he turned around, looked to the back of the church, and saw the boy coming up the road. The African American sermon is experiential.[16]

Therefore, the complication of the sermon is crucial to its efficacy not only in terms of being true to the spirit of Black sacred rhetorical tradition but also with regard to how effectively transformative the sermon is for its hearers. Here is the drama, here is the tragedy, here are elucidated the mundane, quotidian circumstances and existential crises that come to bear in tangible and consequential ways during the preaching moment.

Next, there is the resolution. The resolution furnishes an apt response to the challenges of the complication, principally with the good news of the gospel. It is here that there is the first glimmer of hope to the foundational subject matter of the situation and the tragic-comic and suspenseful commitments of the complication, which ultimately has a view towards the apex of the sermon, the "celebration of the resolution of the suspense. The preacher must celebrate the gospel resolution to the complication."[17] It is during this ecstatic high point, this celebration, that "the Holy Spirit intensifies in core belief to the degree that it can shift perspective, attitude, feeling, and commitment."[18] And this is the most significant feature of this theology, a theology of rejoicing—that no matter the situation or the complication of that situation, there is a resolution to the situation that can and must be celebrated. In the SCRC method, celebration is defined as "the culmination of the sermonic design, where a moment is created in which the remembrance of a redemptive past and/or the conviction of a liberated future transforms the events immediately experienced."[19] With that being said, the central question of this essay is "What can be learned from this traditional approach to African American preaching, particularly of the African American preacher's penchant for celebration?"

---

16. Thomas, *They Like to Never Quit*, 2–3.
17. Thomas, *They Like to Never Quit*, 75.
18. Thomas, *They Like to Never Quit*, 77.
19. Thomas, *They Like to Never Quit*, 72.

Likewise, in chapter 5, "Designing for Celebration," Thomas presents a "preaching worksheet" that outlines the most salient questions that every sermon, composed in the style of the African American celebrative sermonic discourse, should ask:

> THE PREACHING WORKSHEET
> 1. What does this passage say to me?
> 2. What does this passage say to the needs of the people in our time?
> 3. What is the "bad news" in the text? What is the "bad news" for our time?
> 4. What is the "good news" in the text? What is the "good news" for our time?
> 5. Behavioral Purpose Statement
> I propose _____ to the end the hearers will _____.
> 6. Strategy for Celebration
>   a. What shall we celebrate?
>   b. How shall we celebrate our response to 6a?
>   c. What materials of celebration shall we use?[20]

The most significant questions for our discussion here arise in the sixth point of the worksheet, Strategy for Celebration: "a. What shall we celebrate? b. How shall we celebrate our response to 6a? c. What materials of celebration shall we use?"

Upon reading these questions regarding strategies for celebration, I was immediately reminded of Socrates's dialogues from Plato's *The Symposium*, how in it Diotima elucidates on the concept of *poiesis*, though never naming the term baldly. Moreover, for the sake of discussion, I have taken some of *The Symposium*'s concepts out of their original context and located them here because it is a book that dialogues about the different forms of *love*. And a theology of rejoicing is, at its best, a practicable way of dealing with the ills and effects of white supremacy, without mandating retributive action. It is a love theology. Retribution stipulates an eye for an eye sensibility that is ultimately not constructive but rather seeks to inflict harm where harm was inflicted. It is "fatally flawed from a normative viewpoint—sometimes incoherent, sometimes based on bad values, and especially poisonous when people use it to deflect attention from real problems that they feel powerless to solve." A theology of rejoicing strives towards an inductive and imaginative way of constructing new avenues of futurity, the making of a newer world not built upon rectificatory vengeance but restorative justice. This is a point that Fanon relayed in this unmistakably exhortative way:

20. Thomas, *They Like to Never Quit*, 97.

> The notion of catching up must not be used as a pretext to brutalize man, to tear him from himself and his inner consciousness, to break him, to kill him.

Adding:

> No, we do not want to catch up with anyone. But what we want is to walk in the company of man, every man, night and day, for all times. It is not a question of stringing the caravan out where groups are spaced so far apart they cannot see the one in front, and men who no longer recognize each other, meet less and less and talk to each other less and less.

Concluding:

> The Third World must start over a new history of man which takes account of not only the occasional prodigious theses maintained by Europe but also its crimes, the most heinous of which have been committed at the very heart of man, the pathological dismembering of his community, the fracture, the stratification and the bloody tensions fed by class, and finally, on the immense scale of humanity, the racial hatred, slavery, exploitation and, above all, a bloodless genocide whereby one and a half billion men have been written off. So comrades, let us not pay tribute to Europe by creating states, institutions, and societies that draw their inspiration from it. *Humanity expects other things from us than this grotesque and generally obscene emulation.*

And finally:

> If we want to transform Africa into a new Europe, America into a new Europe, then let us entrust the destinies of our countries to the Europeans. They will do a better job than the best of us. But if we want humanity to take one step forward, if we want to take it to another level than the one where Europe has placed it, then we must innovate, *we must be pioneers.*[21]

We must be pioneers. There is new territory within the human consciousness for us to launch expeditions into—new ways of approaching justice, new ways of developing theology, new ways of responding to hurt, new ways of dealing with inequity. The dubious exemplar set by the dominant class, who seek to maintain the status quo, who uphold the religion of white supremacy both directly and indirectly, can never be our model for how we execute our autonomy. And let us be clear, whenever there are those

---

21. Fanon, *Wretched of the Earth*, 308–09.

among us who say they want to *maintain the status quo* or that we *should not disrupt the status quo*, what they are referring to is an old Latin phrase, *status quo res erant ante bellum*, which means "in the state in which things were before the war." It was said to only be used so that each side in the war could maintain their property and rights just the way they were before the great conflict. When it comes to America, the bloodiest war on this soil is the American Civil War, and before the Civil War, Black people did not own any property or territory or have any legal rights. So, when I hear, as a Black man, people say that the status quo is amenable and that we should all work to maintain it; when I hear people say MAKE AMERICA GREAT AGAIN, the implicature therein is that there are those among us, mainly white people, who would use this highly codified languaging to denote how they would like things to go back to the way they were when Black people were the most subjugated and terrorized people in the country (though in many ways we still are). Nevertheless, we Black people do not become terrorists, though we have been subjected to various forms of terror for four hundred years. We do not become nihilists, though for many of us hope is a figment of our imagination, dancing alight in the unimpeachable distance. Rather, we fight using the tools of love, not of oppression and repression, but of righteousness and mercy, which optatively will lead to justice, for love is always "breathing might" into heroes.[22] This is the time for heroic imagination that can inspire hope into the most desperate situations of our times:

As I write this, the world is being ravaged by a deadly viral pandemic. COVID–19, a highly infectious novel coronavirus that has its pathogenesis in the Wuhan province of China, has, reportedly as of this moment, infected over 2.59 million people worldwide, killing over 128,000 people in just six months.[23] The virus has been the catalyst for what is an unprecedented and unbearable series of tragedies, spurring a moment of austere, bleak uncertainty worldwide. This pandemic reminds me of the dialogue between Pausanias and Socrates as relayed to Plato by Aristodemus at the famous symposium. It is Pausanias's turn to speak at his most eloquent about love, and he submits to the party's convivial attendants that there are two types of love: the first type of love is heavenly love (this may also be called Platonic love by some). This is love that is unto "the goddess," in which there is an attraction to another based upon that other's intelligence (we could also infer the other's character and spirit), a unilateral love, which, being a proper motivation to pursue love, makes it good love. The second type of love Pausanias calls "common love." This type, the lower type of love, is

---

22. Plato, *Symposium*, 179b.
23. "Coronavirus World Map."

"genuinely 'common' and undiscriminating in its effects [where] people . . . are attracted . . . to bodies rather than minds."[24] Pausanias goes on to reveal that there are two types of love because the goddess, Aphrodite, is inseparable from *love* and that there are "two kinds of Aphrodite":[25]

> If there was a single Aphrodite, there would be a single Love; but since there are two kinds of Aphrodite, there must also be two Loves. And surely there are *two* kinds of Aphrodite? One of these is older and is the daughter of Uranus, though she has no mother: we call her Uranian or *Heavenly* Aphrodite. The younger one is the daughter of Zeus and Dione: we call her *Pandemic* or *Common* Aphrodite. *So it follows that each type of Love should have the same name of the goddess whose partner he is, and be called Heavenly or Common too.*[26]

Common Aphrodite, called Pandemic, is the source goddess of common love, which is self-seeking, superficial, conceited, vain, vacuous, not genuine, and ultimately destructive. And I submit that, as we seek to build and fashion a just world, if we are animated by love that is not genuine, that is not heavenly, we engage in a spurious love tantamount to a pandemic that will have lasting social, economic, and political consequences, the harms of which will torment us for years to come. As pioneers, we are to be after the construction of a just society, unifying and uplifting disparaged communities, and that work must begin with good theology, a love theology, like a theology of rejoicing.

Nevertheless, because of its similarity of philosophical commitment, there is a Platonic idea (poiesis) that I find useful in not only clarifying Thomas's relevant questions of the what, the how, and the materials of celebration, but also in uncovering newer ways to delve into the pivotal role of celebration in a theology of rejoicing. Thus, the structure of this theology of rejoicing is threefold, extending Thomas's explications, making use of a Platonic concept that redounds to its generative powers: therefore, before I introduce the what (kenosis) and the how (catharsis) of celebration, I need to explain poiesis and what inspired this avenue of understanding the materials of celebration, revisioning what those materials could be. For my purposes here, poiesis contains both kenosis and catharsis, and is the bulwark of the materials of celebration; for my purposes here, the what and the how and the materials are all under the umbrella term, poiesis.

---

24. Plato, *Symposium*, 181b.
25. Plato, *Symposium*, 180d.
26. Plato, *Symposium*, 180e; italics added.

In *The Symposium*, Socrates recounts a discussion he had with Diotima about love and how she influenced his position on the subject. She is the one who taught him that if love is defined (as it was earlier in the night by Agathon) as being both *of* and *desiring of*, then love could not *be* beauty, because if love *were* beauty then it would not *be of* beauty and still have a need *to desire* beauty, because it would already *be* beauty; rather, love, according to Diotima, occurs in the interstitial, metaxological space betwixt *being of* and *being after* something. Through this line of reasoning, as Socrates recounts the conversation, Diotima is brought to the conclusion that all people have love as desire and that that desire is largely towards being immortalized. The principal way that people are immortalized as detailed by Diotima is through their offspring. This love that people have for their offspring, as she comes to explain, is actually empty and devoid of sincerity, that it is all in pursuit of *constructing* something, in this case, constructing immortality:

> You can see the same principle at work if you look at the way people love honour. You'd be amazed at your own stupidity if you failed to see the point of what I've said, after considering how terribly they are affected by love of becoming famous "and storing up immortal fame for eternity." They are readier even to risk every danger for this than for their children's sake . . . . I think it is undying virtue and glorious fame of this sort that motivates everyone in all they do, and the better they are, the more true this is; it's immortality they are in love with.[27]

This is love as libidinous motivator, and it is constructive towards the edification of something that had not existed before—for the subject involved—immortality. Thus, it is using poiesis. This libidinal capacity is ever toward securing a future and is enacted by those who "are pregnant in mind—. . . who are even more pregnant in their minds than in their bodies, and are pregnant with what it is suitable for a mind to bear and bring to birth."[28] There abides in each of us, for whatever reason we may choose to use it, a creative capacity to make something with the lasting power of immortality, a future that looks remarkably different from the way the present moment looks. We are gravid with possibility. A highly constructive enterprise, how we arrive at the possibility theologically is the central and unifying aim of a theology of rejoicing. The following three terms are an exploration of how poiesis may look in this theology: kenosis, catharsis, and, finally, poiesis:

Kenosis: This is the *what* of the celebration. Here is when the supplicant/parishioner prompts/allows an internalization of God's goodness

27. Plato, *Symposium*, 208c.
28. Plato, *Symposium*, 209a.

in times of trouble, compartmentalization of misdeeds, failures, triumphs, successes, traumas—an emptying out of these accidentals, incidentals, circumstances of the self. There is great oneness here, a unity of these experiential modalities as scant and worthless in the light of all that God has accomplished in and through the subject, and in that light a yielding emerges through the action of emptying. This is like Jesus in the garden of Gethsemane submitting himself to bear the brutalism of the cross, or like Christ on the cross, pouring himself out, giving up the ghost.

Catharsis: This is the *how* of the celebration. Through the first instantiation of *kenosis*, there arises a sense of cleansing or purity. This is where rejoicing takes on its purificatory modality/form of expression and affect, releasing the subject from the psychological penalty/burden of mistakes, errors, hurts, grievances in the milieu of encumbrances, both potential and kinetic. It is an ablution or removal of the dregs of the long day, the dour of the destitution that plagues communities of color through the evil effect of white supremacy and thereby releases a moment of clarity that allows for . . .

Poiesis: This is where the *materials* of celebration are explored. Here is the construction of a new future, a recharacterization of a new present, predicated by the thematization of the past. Now it is that we see how "celebration is the culmination . . ., where, by application of the gospel to the complication of life, a moment is created in which remembrance of a redemptive past and/or the conviction of a liberated future transforms the present reality."[29] It is here that I am enabled as the member of a marginalized community, after having emptied out myself of myself, of my will, after having gone through the catharsis brought on by kenosis, that I am now empowered, through my resistance of rejoicing, to construct a future. This is the pivotal point of rejoicing. This is the most prominent and profound feature as seen in the tradition of Black sacred rhetoric, that no matter how my life has begun, it can still end in celebration and rejoicing. That there may be a situation and a complication and the resolution of those two sermonic components held in tension may not seem to be redemptive at all for me, but I can still shout. In the midst of my turmoil, I can still glory. This is what is meant in the vernacular of the Black church: "When praises go up, blessings come down." How do we qualify blessings? Is it about strictly material successes and possessions, or is it something deeper? This is what intense joy, better known as rejoicing, looks like in practice. This is what weaponized joy looks like—to confront that which affronts you as a member of a disparaged community on a daily basis with joy, with aplomb, with a theology of rejoicing.

---

29. Thomas, *They Like to Never Quit*, 80.

A CONTRAST OF POEMS

And so, I choose to rejoice. I choose to rejoice even in the ugly moments, moments which in themselves are a brand of death, a morbidity. A theology of rejoicing is a highly moral act because it does not predicate a precipitate response that is steeped in the violence that it received. It is constructive. It does not lash out but looks within—to *kenotically* remove myself from all humiliation and responsibility in the moment—to *cathartically* rid myself of any animosity towards those who offended me, coming to a clarity that I was in no way deserving of the affronting, that it still happened, that I should not respond with the violence intuitive of the violence I received—and to *poietically* confront and rejoinder the oppressive act by joying regardless, as one standing in the present yet in the future, in a day removed from the dark of oppression. If this all still sounds too theoretical and optimistic, perhaps a study in poetry will help illumine my meaning.

There are two poems which, when contrasted for their most essential parts, evince what the focal point of a theology of rejoicing, *poiesis*, looks like in practice. First, there is Langston Hughes's classic verse, a comment on the failure of the evolution of equalizing the races in America, musing over the belayed trajectory of the Black person, from antebellum to the early twentieth century, "I, Too," the high point of which is as follows:

> Tomorrow,
> I'll be at the table
> When company comes.
> Nobody'll dare
> Say to me,
> "Eat in the kitchen,"
> Then.
> Besides,
> They'll see how beautiful I am
> And be ashamed—"[30]

I dislike this poem. Not for the razor-edged ingenuity in resembling twentieth-century slice-of-life Black America with the horrors of the ancestral experience of the plantation enslavement, not for the bustling images, teeming with verve. For cultivating a profitable future, this poem is not useful for two reasons: 1) Why is the vaunted symbol of the poem, "the table," the speaker's motivation, this artifact representative of a destructive hegemonic power structure that precludes some whilst inviting others? Moreover, why should he/does he feel that he needs be at the table that reviles his

---

30. Hughes, "I, Too" from *Collected Poems*, 46.

very being? Why does the speaker not endeavor to construct his own table? 2) The poem espouses what I term *compulsory eschatological positivism*, that is, for the oppressed it must always be tomorrow—"Tomorrow, I'll be at the table when company comes." It must always be tomorrow for the oppressed person, because today for them is never sufficient. There is the sense that it *must* be tomorrow. For the Black person living in America, it has always been necessary that he or she has hope in a tomorrow, and for the Black person in America this is no longer sagacious or satisfactory.

Note the insistence by the speaker/subject of the poem and his reliance upon the supposed good will of the object of the poem, those who, peradventure the encounter of the turning of their hearts, will somehow see how beautifully human Black people have been all along and allow the Black person a seat at the table. What utter nonsense! It is quite reminiscent of Vasko's hope in *A Theology for Bystanders* that somehow or another those in positions of power will hear the cry of the oppressed and suddenly, at long last, relinquish their power. Acceptable in its time and epoch, this tomorrow, though blithe and sanguine, is not a constructive tomorrow; though this is often perceived to be the tomorrow ensconced in Black sacred rhetoric, it is no longer sufficient for Black people. This is because it lacks the prophetic features of what I term the *tomorrow of poiesis*.

That trait is found in another poem by yet another important Black poet, Lucille Clifton, found in this excerpt of her poem, "Won't You Celebrate with Me":

> won't you celebrate with me
> what i have shaped into
> a kind of life? i had no model....
> i made it up ...
> my one hand holding tight
> my other hand; come celebrate
> with me that everyday
> something has tried to kill me
> and has failed.[31]

Here we see the constructive capacity of poiesis on full display. It upends the expected outcomes of dragooning and oppressive social normatives of white supremacist society; it is entirely intrepid in how it constantly looks to generate a newness of self despite having no precursor of selfhood upon which to model itself. Indeed, it is a tomorrow enclosed in a today. This is the tomorrow of poiesis—an ex nihilo expression of futurity construction embedded in a theology that celebrates the victory that is selfhood as life,

---

31. Clifton, "Won't You Celebrate with Me."

where there should be only death and disparagement. I may be a woman, I may be Black, I may be gay, I may be trans—I may be on the very margins of society—but there is a call towards a celebration, a rejoicing that envisages a possibility of productivity and prosperity even in the broken community. Hear her say, "Come celebrate with me that everyday something has tried to kill me and has failed." It, this celebration, the peroration of the sermonic speech act transposed to the peroration of the lived act, is communal at its most fundamental level. This is key because community is central to how we experience the world around us, a point Paul Tillich discusses in *The Courage to Be*:

> The world as a whole is potential, not actual. Those sections are actual with which one is partially identical. The more self-relatedness a being has the more it is able, according to the polar structure of reality, to participate. Man as the completely centered being or as a person can participate in everything, but he participates through that section of the world which makes him a person. Only in the continuous encounter with other persons does the person become and remain a person. The place of this encounter is the community. Man's participation in nature is direct, insofar as he is a definite part of nature through his bodily existence. His participation in nature is indirect and mediated through the community insofar as he transcends nature by knowing and shaping it.[32]

Consequently, it becomes apparent, if it is true that community is the apparatus through which we not only are enabled to interact with the world around us, but by which we are assisted in substantiating our very personhood, then the relevant questions become, "What of the communities that are disparaged? What about communities, particularly communities of color, that are broken through years of systemic denigration and systematic degradation? What chance do they have to participate in the world as complete and well-orbed beings?"

Enter the culmination of a theology of rejoicing: that there is a fellowship of celebration as a witness to the promise that God, a God who is on the side of the oppressed, has deposited in each of us—that there is construction that can occur right now that can ensure the desirable outcomes of the future, that there need be no blithe, blind optimism—tomorrow can be actualized today. This is the tomorrow of poiesis. This is the promise of a theology of rejoicing.

---

32. Tillich, *Courage to Be*, 127.

Coda

BELOVED COMMUNITY

Last night

I had a dream
that we processioned out
after the morning service
the ivory sunlight of open doors
weighing heavy on
chilled bones
(a siege of air conditioning
when church fans
only feed the insatiable
summer pew)

and seated in the vestibule
of all people
was Gwendolyn Brooks
and Ms. Brooks sat by just
watching

greetings laden with kiss, honeyed with
the belly song of laughter

greetings noisy as high noon

galloping heart to heart
each embrace unfraught, untethered to
despair

gallivanting guffaws falling
between
aches aging knees
smiles older than pain

blue dresses humming
against indigo skin
double breasted suits, peaking lapels
ashen hands outstretched
clasping tightly
another's

the familiar music of hand clap
back pat pat

the familial vaunted pitch of
asking about mothers
how the brother is doing
where the son is now
is the daughter well
when is father
returning

where we going to eat
who driving
echoing uproarious

leaving and staying

and finally
she spoke

from the edge of her galaxy
Ms. Brooks
eyes darkened with sage
words finding audience
just above a whisper
louder than justice

"This, right here, is the most important thing to us."

This, right here, is the most important thing to us.

This, right here, is the most important thing.

Glossary

"PREACHING AND JUSTICE"

1. Theology—a person's orientation towards God's hand in the furtherance of the human project.

2. Locutionary—the speech act itself, an utterance that is understandable and perceivable by the hearer.

3. Illocutionary—the intent behind the words of a speech act, i.e., the word's intended logics.

4. Perlocutionary—Paul Ricœur defines the perlocutionary act of speech as that part of speech which has an intended, often emotive, effect in the hearer of the words.

"WHITE SUPREMACY IS A RELIGION"

5. Ontological Indexicality—a term taken from the annals of Peircean terminology, from his concept of *index*, meaning the quality of one's own being and what points to that specific being existing as it is.

Bibliography

Alexander, Michelle. *The New Jim Crow: Mass Incarceration in the Age of Colorblindness.* New York: New, 2012.

Anderson, Victor. *Beyond Ontological Blackness: An Essay on African American Religious and Cultural Criticism.* New York: Continuum International, 1995.

Bakhtin, Mikhail. *Toward a Philosophy of the Act.* Austin: University of Texas Press, 1993.

Baldwin, James. *Fire Next Time.* New York: Dial, 1963.

Beauvoir, Simone de. *The Second Sex.* London: Random House, 2009.

Bennett, Joshua. *Being Property Once Myself: Blackness and the End of Man.* Cambridge, MA: Harvard University Press, 2020.

Biography.com Editors. "Theodore Roosevelt." https://www.biography.com/us-president/theodore-roosevelt.

Bouie, Jamelle. "Michael Brown Wasn't a Superhuman Demon." *Slate*, Nov. 26, 2014. https://slate.com/news-and-politics/2014/11/darren-wilsons-racial-portrayal-of-michael-brown-as-a-superhuman-demon-the-ferguson-police-officers-account-is-a-common-projection-of-racial-fears.html.

Booth, Robert and Caelainn Barr. "Black People Four Times More Likely to Die from Covid-19, ONS Finds." *Guardian*, May 7, 2020. https://www.theguardian.com/world/2020/may/07/black-people-four-times-more-likely-to-die-from-covid-19-ons-finds.

Bourdieu, Pierre. *The Logic of Practice.* Stanford, CA: Stanford University Press, 1990.

Brooks, Gwendolyn. "Paul Robeson." https://poets.org/poem/paul-robeson.

Brown, DeNeen L. "Hunting Down Runaway Slaves: The Cruel Ads of Andrew Jackson and 'The Master Class.'" *Washington Post*, May 1, 2017. https://www.washingtonpost.com/news/retropolis/wp/2017/04/11/hunting-down-runaway-slaves-the-cruel-ads-of-andrew-jackson-and-the-master-class/.

Brueggemann, Walter. *The Word Militant: Preaching a Decentering Word.* Minneapolis: Fortress, 2007.

Bultmann, Rudolf Karl. *New Testament and Mythology and Other Basic Writings.* Edited and translated by Schubert M. Ogen. Philadelphia: Fortress, 1984.

Burns, Ric, dir. *New York: A Documentary Film.* DVD. New York: Steeplechase Films, 1999.

Cannon, Katie Geneva. *Katie's Canon: Womanism and the Soul of the Black Community.* New York: Continuum, 1998.

———. *Teaching Preaching: Isaac Rufus Clark and Black Sacred Rhetoric.* New York: Continuum, 2003.

Cavanaugh, William T. *Torture and Eucharist: Theology, Politics, and the Body of Christ.* Hoboken, NJ: Wiley-Blackwell, 1998.

Cartwright, Samuel A. "Report on the Diseases and Peculiarities of the Negro Race." *DeBow's Review,* 1851.

Chesnutt, Charles W. "The Wife of His Youth." In *The Norton Anthology of African American Literature,* edited by Henry Louis Gates Jr. and Nellie Y. McKay, 545–53. New York: W. W. Norton, 1997.

Clifton, Lucille. "Won't You Celebrate with Me." Poetry Foundation. https://www.poetryfoundation.org/poems/50974/wont-you-celebrate-with-me.

Coates, Ta-Nehisi. *Between the World and Me.* New York: Random House, 2015.

Cone, James Hal. *The Cross and the Lynching Tree.* Ossining, NY: Orbis, 2013.

"Confederate Monuments in Virginia." www.vpap.org. Article discontinued.

"Coronavirus World Map: Tracking the Global Outbreak." https://www.nytimes.com/interactive/2021/world/covid-cases.amp.html.

"Crime in the United States 2019." https://ucr.fbi.gov/crime-in-the-u.s/2019/crime-in-the-u.s.-2019/topic-pages/tables/table-43.

Crowell, Steven. "Existentialism." In *The Stanford Encylopedia of Philosophy,* Aug. 23, 2004; rev. June 9, 2020. Metaphysics Research Lab, Center for the Study of Language and Information, Stanford University. https://plato.stanford.edu/entries/existentialism/.

Desmond, Matthew. *Evicted: Poverty and Profit in the American City.* New York: Broadway, 2017.

Douglas, Kelly Brown. *Stand Your Ground: Black Bodies and the Justice of God.* Ossining, NY: Orbis, 2015.

———. *What's Faith Got to Do with It? Black Bodies/Christian Souls.* Ossining, NY: Orbis, 1995.

Douglass, Frederick. "What, to the Slave, Is the Fourth of July?" In *Great Speeches by African Americans,* by James Daley. Mineola, NY: Dover, 2006.

Downey, Tom. "The Beau Brummels of Brazzaville." *Wall Street Journal,* Sept. 29, 2011. https://www.wsj.com/articles/SB10001424053111903927204576574553723025760.

Du Bois, W. E. B. *The Souls of Black Folk.* Chicago: McClurg, 1903.

Fanon, Frantz. *The Wretched of the Earth.* New York: Grove, 1963.

Ferguson, Robert A. "Michael Brown, Ferguson, and the Ghosts of Pruitt-Igoe." *Cultural Critique* 90 (Spring 2015) 140–44.

Foucault, Michel. *Ethics: Subjectivity and Truth.* Edited by Paul Rabinow. Essential Works of Foucault 1. New York: New, 1998.

Franklin, Ronald. "How Abraham Lincoln Fired General John C. Fremont." *Owlcation,* June 17, 2019. https://owlcation.com/humanities/How-Abraham-Lincoln-Fired-General-John-C-Fremont.

Gates, Henry Louis, Jr. *Stony the Road: Reconstruction, White Supremacy, and The Rise of Jim Crow.* New York: Penguin, 2019.

"George Washington and Teeth from Enslaved People." https://www.mountvernon.org/george-washington/health/washingtons-teeth/george-washington-and-slave-teeth/.

Glass, Andrew. "Theodore Roosevelt Reviews Race Relations, Feb. 13, 1905." *Politico*, Feb. 13, 2017. https://www.politico.com/story/2017/02/theodore-roosevelt-reviews-race-relations-feb-13-1905-234938.

Gordon-Reed, Annette. *Thomas Jefferson and Sally Hemings: An American Controversy.* Charlottesville, VA: University of Virginia Press, 1998.

Green, Erica L. "Why Are Black Students Punished So Often?: Minnesota Confronts a National Quandary." *New York Times*, Mar. 3, 2018. https://www.nytimes.com/2018/03/18/us/politics/school-discipline-disparities-white-black-students.html.

Harris, James Henry. *Preaching Liberation*. Minneapolis: Augsburg, 1995.

Hayden, Robert. *Collected Poems*. New York: Liveright, 1962.

Heidegger, Martin. *Being and Time*. Translated by John Macquarrie and Edward Robinson. Reprint, Oxford: Blackwell, 2001. http://pdf-objects.com/files/Heidegger-Martin-Being-and-Time-trans.-Macquarrie-Robinson-Blackwell-1962.pdf.

Hughes, Langston. *The Collected Poems of Langston Hughes*. Edited by Arnold Rampersad. New York: Vintage Classics, 1995.

Hurst, Charles E. *Social Inequality: Forms, Causes, and Consequences*. 6th ed. Boston: Allyn and Bacon, 2007.

Johnson, Akilah. "Boston. Racism. Image. Reality." *Boston Globe*, Dec. 10, 2017. https://apps.bostonglobe.com/spotlight/boston-racism-image-reality/series/image/.

Kaeble, Danielle and Lauren E. Glaze. "Correctional Populations in the United States, 2013." Dec. 2014. Bureau of Justice Statistics. https://www.bjs.gov/content/pub/pdf/cpus13.pdf.

Kant, Immanuel. *Observations on the Feeling of the Beautiful and Sublime*. Translated by John T. Goldthwait. Berkeley: University of California Press, 2004.

Krebs, Christopher. *A Most Dangerous Book: Tacitus's Germania from the Roman Empire to the Third Reich*. New York: Norton, 2012.

Laborde, Cécile. *Liberalism's Religion*. Cambridge, MA: Harvard University Press, 2017.

Lai, K. K. Rebecca, et al. "Is America's Military Big Enough?" *New York Times*, Mar. 22, 2017. https://www.nytimes.com/interactive/2017/03/22/us/is-americas-military-big-enough.html.

León, Felice. "The National Anthem Is Racist, and We Made a Video in Case You Forgot." *Root*, July 4, 2018. https://www.theroot.com/the-national-anthem-is-racist-and-we-made-a-video-in-c-1827329501.

"Lincoln on Slavery." National Park Service. https://www.nps.gov/liho/learn/historyculture/slavery.htm.

Lipsitz, George. "From *Plessy* to Ferguson." *Cultural Critique* 90 (Spring 2015) 119–39.

Lopez, German. "Police Officers Are Prosecuted for Murder in Less Than Two Percent of Fatal Shootings." *Vox*, updated Apr. 2, 2021. https://www.vox.com/21497089/derek-chauvin-george-floyd-trial-police-prosecutions-black-lives-matter.

———. "There Are Huge Racial Disparities in How US Police Use Force." *Vox*, updated Nov. 14, 2018. http://www.vox.com/identities/2016/8/13/17938186/police-shootings-killings-racism-racial-disparities.

Marx, Karl and Friedrich Engels. *The Communist Manifesto*. New York: Simon and Schuster, 1964.

Meinong, Alexius. "The Theory of Objects." In *Realism and the Background of Phenomenology*, by Roderick M. Chisholm. N.p.: n.p., 1960.

NAACP. *Criminal Justice Fact Sheet.* https://www.naacp.org/criminal-justice-fact-sheet/.
Neely, Priska. *Black Babies Twice as Likely as White Babies To Die Before Age One.* Transcript from *Weekend Edition Sunday.* NPR, July 8, 2018. https://www.npr.org/2018/07/08/627024896/black-babies-twice-as-likely-as-white-babies-to-die-before-age-1.
Nelson, Raina. "Black Women and the Pay Gap." *AAUW,* August 1, 2018. https://www.aauw.org/article/black-women-and-the-pay-gap/.
Nussbaum, Martha C. *The Monarchy of Fear: A Philosopher Looks at Our Political Crisis.* New York: Simon & Schuster, 2018.
Patrick, Robert. "Darren Wilson's Radio Calls Show Fatal Encounter Was Brief." *St. Louis Post-Dispatch,* November 14, 2014. https://www.stltoday.com/news/multimedia/special/darren-wilsons-radio-calls-show-fatal-encounter-was-brief/html_79c17aed-0dbe-514d-ba32-bad908056790.html.
Peck, Raoul. *I Am Not Your Negro.* N.p.: Amazon Studios, 2017.
Peirce, Charles S. "On a New List of Categories." *Proceedings of the American Academy of Arts and Sciences* 7 (1867) 278–89.
Plato. *The Symposium.* Edited and translated by Christopher Gill. New York: Penguin Classics. 1999.
"Police Shootings Database, 2015–2021." https://www.washingtonpost.com/graphics/investigations/police-shootings-database/.
Porterfield, Carlie. "Trump Claims He's Done More for Blacks than Any President Besides Lincoln." *Forbes,* June 12, 2020. https://www.forbes.com/sites/carlieporterfield/2020/06/12/trump-claims-hes-done-more-for-blacks-than-any-president-besides-lincoln/?sh=5fdf2e22c208.
"Portsmouth, VA: Crime Rates." https://www.neighborhoodscout.com/va/portsmouth/crime#data.
Pound, Marcus. *Žižek: A (Very) Critical Introduction.* Grand Rapids: Eerdmans, 2008.
———. *The Žižek Reader.* Edited by Elizabeth Wright and Edmond Leo Wright. Oxford, UK: Blackwell, 1999.
Randolph, Sarah N. *The Domestic Life of Thomas Jefferson: Compiled from Family Letters and Reminiscences by His Great-Granddaughter, Sarah N. Randolph.* Cambridge, MA: University Press, 1939.
Rankine, Claudia. *Citizen: An American Lyric.* Minneapolis: Graywolf, 2014.
Ricœur, Paul. *Interpretation Theory: Discourse and the Surplus of Meaning.* Fort Worth: Texas Christian University Press, 1976.
Saraiya, Sonya. "Viola Davis: 'My Entire Life Has Been a Protest.'" *Vanity Fair,* July 14, 2020. https://www.vanityfair.com/hollywood/2020/07/cover-story-viola-davis.
Sartre, Jean-Paul. *Existentialism Is a Humanism.* Reprint, New Haven, CT: Yale University Press, 2007.
Sleeth, Ronald E. *Proclaiming the Word.* Nashville: Abingdon, 1964.
"Ten Facts about Washington and Slavery." https://www.mountvernon.org/george-washington/slavery/ten-facts-about-washington-slavery/.
Thomas, Frank A. *They Like to Never Quit Praisin' God: The Role of Celebration in Preaching.* Rev. ed. Cleveland: Pilgrim, 1997.
Tillich, Paul. *The Courage to Be.* New Haven, CT: Yale University Press, 1952.

Tippett, Krista. "Ruby Sales: Where Does It Hurt?" *On Being* radio interview, Sept. 15, 2016, updated Jan. 16, 2020. https://onbeing.org/programs/ruby-sales-where-does-it-hurt/.

Trump, Donald. "Remarks by President Trump at South Dakota's 2020 Mount Rushmore Fireworks Celebration: Keystone, South Dakota." July 4, 2020. White House. https://trumpwhitehouse.archives.gov/briefings-statements/remarks-president-trump-south-dakotas-2020-mount-rushmore-fireworks-celebration-keystone-south-dakota/.

Tucker, Abigail. "Digging up the Past at a Richmond Jail." *Smithsonian Magazine*, March 2009. https://www.smithsonianmag.com/history/digging-up-the-past-at-a-richmond-jail-50642859/.

Turner, Victor. *The Forest of Symbols: Aspects of Ndembe Ritual*. Ithaca, NY: Cornell University Press, 1970.

Vasko, Elisabeth T. *Beyond Apathy: A Theology for Bystanders*. Minneapolis: Fortress, 2015.

Weaver, Afaa Michael. "American Income." www.poetryfoundation.org/poetrymagazine/poems/49296/american-income.

West, Cornel. *Race Matters*. Boston: Beacon, 1993.

———. *Prophetic Reflections: Notes on Race and Power in America*. Monroe, ME: Common Courage, 1993.

Wilson, August. *Seven Guitars*. New York: Penguin, 1996.

Yuen, Helen and Asantewa Boakyewa. "The African American Girl Who Helped Make the Star-Spangled Banner." National Museum of American History, May 30, 2014. https://americanhistory.si.edu/blog/2014/05/the-african-american-girl-who-helped-make-the-star-spangled-banner.html.

Žižek, Slavoj. *The Sublime Object of Ideology*. New York: Verso, 2009.

www.ingramcontent.com/pod-product-compliance
Lightning Source LLC
Chambersburg PA
CBHW050835160426
43192CB00010B/2029